Crossroads Alaska

Native Cultures of Alaska and Siberia

Valérie Chaussonnet

Arctic Studies Center
National Museum of Natural History
Smithsonian Institution
Washington, D.C.

1995

*Captions indicate the largest
dimension, of the height, length, width,
or diameter of the artifact.*

Cover Photos:

Back Cover.

*Udegei shaman's
drum cover from
Khor River, Amur
River region, Russia,
from the late 1800s.
Made of birch bark,
cotton, pigment, and
leather. Vladivostok
Maritime Museum,
Russia, #2180-8a.
74 cm. See also
p. 73.*

Bottom Center.

*Asian Eskimo
float plug from Big
Diomede Island,
Russia, collected in
1885 by F.K. Gek,
made of wood and
blue glass beads for
the eyes. Vladivostok
Maritime Museum,
Russia, #1132-34. 7
cm. See also p. 93.*

Botton Right.

*Athapaskan (Ingalik)
night and day mask
from the Kuskokwim
River, Alaska, 1879,
made of wood, pig-
ments, and feathers.
National Museum
of Natural History,
Smithsonian
Institution,
#E64242. 47 cm.
See also p. 74.*

Top Left.

*Western Thule culture
(Eskimo) ivory
woman with hair in
bun, collected in
Punuk Island,
Alaska, by Henry B.
Collins in 1929,
dated at about A.D.
1000. #A342783.
3.7 cm. See also
p. 65.*

Middle Left.

*Ulchi Khaka doll
made from paper,
yarn, and fabric, by
G. Kuisali, Amur
River, Siberia, 1991.
The body with the
head is inserted into
a slit in the dress at
the neck. Khabarovsk
Regional Museum,
Russia, #VX3/14.
12 cm. See also p. 57.*

Inside Front Cover.

*Udegei shaman-
ancestor figure
riding his helping
spirit, collected in
1959 by V.G. Lar'kin
in the village of
Gvasiugi. The wood-
en shaman is dressed
in leather and fur.
This is a powerful
protector for the prac-
ticing shaman, as it
represents a shaman
traveling to the world
of spirits on the back
of his helping spirit, a
tiger-like beast.
Vladivostok
Maritime Museum,
Russia, #4511-19.
35.5 cm (beast) and
27 cm (shaman).
See also p. 75.*

Inside Back Cover.

*Tlingit shaman with
dagger and typically
long shaman's hair
style, from the late
1800s. National
Museum of Natural
History, Smithsonian
Institution,
E73837. 24 cm.
See also p. 72.*

Chaussonnet, Valérie

Crossroads Alaska: native cultures of Alaska
and Siberia / Valérie Chaussonnet.

112 pp.   21.59 x 29.68 cm.

Includes bibliographical references.

1. Eskimos – Alaska – Material culture –
Exhibitions. 2. Eskimos – Russia – Siberia –
Material culture – Exhibitions. 3. Indians of
North America – Alaska – Material culture –
Exhibitions. 4. Eskimo art – Alaska–
Exhibitions. 5. Eskimo art – Russia –
Siberia – Exhibitions. 6. Indian Art –Alaska
– Exhibitions. I. Title.

E99.E7C525   1995
979.8'004971–dc20
95–804
CIP

This catalogue is set in Adobe Garamond
and Futura Bold.

Printing: Upstate Litho
Design: Harp and Company

Acknowledgements

Crossroads Alaska was born out of a larger "Crossroads" concept, which was first developed through the major international exhibition *Crossroads of Continents: Cultures of Siberia and Alaska* (1988-1992), and through a symposium held in Washington, D.C., in September 1988, both under the leadership of the Smithsonian Institution's Arctic Studies Center. Two volumes were published, the exhibition catalogue (edited by William W. Fitzhugh and Aron Crowell), and the acts of the symposium under the title *Anthropology of the North Pacific Rim* (edited by William W. Fitzhugh and Valérie Chaussonnet). The idea for *Crossroads Alaska*, a more compact and easily traveled exhibition, came from regret at being unable to bring the original Crossroads exhibit to locations where the artifacts originated (except, in Alaska, at the Anchorage Museum of History and Art).

Crossroads Alaska was organized by the Arctic Studies Center, National Museum of Natural History, Smithsonian Institution, under the direction of William W. Fitzhugh, and curated by Valérie Chaussonnet.

The exhibition was designed, edited, and produced by the Office of Exhibits Central, Smithsonian Institution, Washington, D.C.

The Alaska tour was coordinated by Coordinator Extraordinaire Jean Flanagan Carlo, Fairbanks, Alaska.

Funding and assistance were provided by: the Alaska Humanities Forum; the Alaska State Council on the Arts; the Alaska State Museums, Juneau, and Sheldon Jackson Museum, Sitka; the Anchorage Museum of History and Art; British Petroleum; the Department of Anthropology, National Museum of Natural History, Smithsonian Institution; the City of Fairbanks Hotel/Motel Bed Tax Fund; the Friends of the Alaska State Museum; the Friends of the University of Alaska Museum; Man and the Biosphere; the National Endowment for the Arts; the National Park Service, Anchorage, and the Beringian International Park project; the National Science Foundation; the Smithsonian Institution Special Exhibition Fund; the University of Alaska Museum, Fairbanks; and Young and Associates.

The lending museums and institutions for the exhibition are: the National Museum of Natural History, Smithsonian Institution, Washington, D.C.; the National Museum of the American Indian, Smithsonian Institution, New York; the University of Alaska Museum, Fairbanks; the Koniag Area Native Association, Kodiak, Alaska; the Arsenev Maritime State Museum, Vladivostok; the Sakhalin Regional Museum, Iuzhno-Sakhalinsk; the Arsenev Regional Museum, Khabarovsk; the Northeastern Interdisciplinary Research Center, Magadan; and the Kamchatka Regional Museum, Petropavlovsk-Kamchatskii.

We wish to acknowledge Russian-American scientific cooperation and friendship in arctic matters, in particular the persistence of the Sakhalin Museum team and the vision of the Arctic Studies Center at the Smithsonian Institution for making this exhibition happen.

For their support, assistance, and encouragement, we wish to thank the following individuals: Brenda Abney, Glenn Adams, Harry Adams, Eduard Efimovich Alekseev, Galina Aleksandrovna Aleksiuk, Helen Alten, Alvin Amason, Terence Armstrong, Sergei Aleksandrovich Arutiunov, Mark O. Badger, James H. Barker, Françoise Barlesi, Hugh Bennett, Steve Bouta, Karen Brewster, Marga Buffard, Pat Burke, Todd Burrier, Vladimir Valer'evich Bychkov, J.B. Bynum, Harold Campbell, Glen and Elena Carlo, Rosemary Carlton, James Carr, Hélène Carrère d'Encausse, Sue Carter, Alex Castro, Wanda Chin, Lora Collins, Peter Corey, Aron Crowell, Liudmila Mikhailovna Danilina, Hazel Daro, Richard and Nora Dauenhauer, Mark Daughhetee, Valerie Davidson, Anatolii Panteleevich Derevianko, Koji Deriha, Dominique Desson, Eileen Devinney, Terry P. Dickey, Edith Dietze, Nikolai N. Dikov, E. James Dixon, Bernadette Driscoll, Nancy Eddy, Sarah Elder, Danny Fielding, Ann Fienup-Riordan, Jean Flanagan Carlo, Joseph Engel, Marnie Forbis, Paul Gardinier, Martine de Gaudemar, Craig Gerlach, Nelson H.H. Graburn, Jana Harcharek, Mike Headley, Steve Henrikson, Gail Hollinger, Chang-su Houchins, Jerry Howard, Karlin Ichoak, Mina A. Jacobs, Teresa John, Aldona Jonaitis, Suzi Jones, Cynthia Jones, Leonard Kammerling, Bruce Kato, Paula Kaufman, Mike Kelton, Basile Kerblay, Gennadii and Tatiana Khokhorin, Richard Kilday, Rich Kleinleder, Richard A. Knecht, Vera Vasil'evna Kobko, Kathryn Kolkhorst Ruddy, Aleksandr K. Koniapatskii, Michael E. Krauss, Holly Krieg, Igor Krupnik, Georgii Gavrilovich Kudelin, Vladislav M. Ladishev, Dinah Larsen, Joe Leahy, Aleksandr Lebedintsev, Molly Lee, Mary-Jane Lenz, Ted Levin, Glenda Lindley, Jon Loring, Eve Macintyre, Martha Madsen, Ron Manook, Reed Martin, Rolando Mayen, Laura McLean, Pamela Moore, Emanuel Morgan, Shirley Moses, Bradford Nageak, David Neakok, Valerie Jean Nelson, David Norton, Victoria Oliver, Aleksandr Oriakov, Darlene Orr, Natalia Pavlovna Otki, Ol'ga Pavlova, Robert Perantoni, Betsy Pitzman, Aleksei K. Ponomarenko, Anna Aleksandrovna Ponomareva, Roger Powers, Andrei Valentinovich Ptashinskii, Gordon L. Pullar, George Quist, Diane Rathman, Rosemary Regan, Chris Reinecke, Carol Reuter, James Reuter, Paul Rhymer, Svetlana Pavlovna Rozhnova, Susan Rowley, Caroline Sadler, Bernard Saladin d'Anglure, Peter and Saltanat Schweitzer, Linda Shea, Valerii Orionovich Shubin, Ol'ga Alekseevna Shubina, John Siske, Sergei Slobodin, Liz Smalls, Tim Smith, Ben Snouffer, Aleksandr Bagmoevich Soktoev, Walter Sorrell, Mary Stachelrodt, Tim Stone, Svetlana Aleksandrovna Tag'ek, Tasian Tein, Sue Thorsen, Ted Timreck, Anton Tynel', Anthony Valentine, Catharine Valentour, Walter VanHorn, Ruslan Sergeevich Vasil'evskii, Igor Vorobei, Alvina Voropaeva, Tibor Waldner, William Walton, Eric Washington, Betsy Webb, Kim Wells, Janet Williams, Pat Wolf, Rosita Worl, Miranda Wright, Kenneth Young, Jocelyn Young, and Jon Zastrow.

Special thanks to my parents Colette and Pierre Chaussonnet, and to my husband Norman R. Dorsett.

This catalogue was edited by Rosemary Regan.
The artifacts were photographed by Carl Hansen and Laurie Penland, National Museum of Natural History, Smithsonian Institution.
Catalogue design by Harp and Company.

A la mémoire de mon ami,
Andris Slapins.

Table of Contents

Preface

William W. Fitzhugh

As originally conceived almost twenty years ago, the Crossroads project was planned as a way to explore and celebrate the shared heritage of the peoples and cultures surrounding Bering Strait. The Russian, Canadian, and American curators who created the original exhibit *Crossroads of Continents: Cultures of Siberia and Alaska* opened a new era of cooperation in research and museum studies across Bering Strait that had been abandoned for more than half a century as a wave of political, ideological, and economic competition swept over the globe. Ironically, nowhere was this clash more evident than along the shores of the North Pacific and Bering Strait, where Native peoples had been in contact for ages before Europeans arrived.

To outsiders this region appeared almost too remarkable for words. Its lands and waters teemed with life, and its peoples had learned to utilize its resources to produce cultures of great vitality and distinctiveness. In the Natives' clothing and skin boats; in their social organization and mythology; and in their art and religion, early explorers and scientists sensed sophistication and complexity. Perhaps most striking, from the European point of view, was Native recognition of a special spiritual link that joined humans, animals, and their homelands in a bond of mutual respect that permeated all aspects of life. Such beliefs, if they had ever been present in Western culture, had fallen prey to human domination thousands of years earlier as people learned to manipulate their environment and imposed an ideology of human control over everything in their path.

That path reached around the globe to the North Pacific from two directions, as Russian Pomors and Cossacks advanced to Bering Strait from the west in the 17th century and as European explorers and whalers advanced from the east in the 18th and 19th centuries. By the mid-20th century, with its peoples racked by Western-introduced diseases and its environment depleted of its most valuable furs and seamammals, Cold War military confrontation and industrial development brought a new wave of external forces into the region. Languages, cultures, and kin were separated on either side of an artificial boundary that Native peoples had never previously recognized.

The same fate befell the early archival and artifact collections gathered by the earliest Westerners who visited these regions. Artifacts documenting the early history of North Pacific peoples, collected by explorers and scientists over two centuries from the 1740s to the 1920s, found themselves on either side of impenetrable political barriers. The greatest collection of early Alaskan artifacts, gathered by the Russian scientist I.G. Voznesenskii from Russian America in the 1840s, had been sent to St Petersburg, where it became inaccessible to Americans. In a corresponding twist of fate, the largest and best-documented collections of northeastern Asia, gathered by Russian anthropologists W. Bogoras and W. Jochelson for the Jesup North Pacific Expedition[1], went to the storerooms of the American Museum of Natural History in New York City, and thereafter were never seen in Russia. Thus Native people as well as the general population of Russia and North America became forever estranged from a major portion of their heritage.

Deprived of the means for learning about the history of Native cultures in their own lands, Americans and Russians on both sides suffered intellectual and aesthetic losses. Throughout the 20th century, as political and economic forces prevailed, it became increasingly difficult for outsiders or Native peoples to see this region as having shared a common past. In the absence of contacts and dialogue across Bering Strait, its peoples began to be seen as separate, alienated, aligned only with their current political states.

The *Crossroads of Continents* exhibit was designed to address this accident of history by combining cultural materials from northeastern Siberia and northwestern North America into a single joint traveling exhibition that could be seen by peoples on both sides of Bering Strait. After nearly a decade of planning, during which our project was interrupted by the Soviet invasion of Afghanistan and the downing of the Korean jetliner, it seemed that we would finally accomplish our goal when the last hurdle, Soviet agreement to display the Crossroads exhibition in the Soviet Union, was cleared in 1987. Shortly after, in 1988, *Crossroads of Continents* opened at the Smithsonian and began a three-year North American tour to Seattle, New York, Indianapolis, Los Angeles, Anchorage, and Ottawa. The show was greeted with great acclaim, and its message of cultural interchange and open borders found resonance in a new-found spirit of openness and political reconciliation of the "glasnost" era.

But just when the Crossroads exhibit was about to complete its tour in North America, new and unforeseen barriers emerged as the economic and social structure of the Soviet Union collapsed, leaving its museums without funds and its transportation and security systems in disarray. Our colleagues at the Institute of Ethnography (Soviet Academy of Sciences) now had more immediate concerns than honoring exhibit agreements; nor could they guarantee the safety of the objects for the planned Russian tour. For a while we thought that the absenceof Russian funds could be solved by American donors, but none could be found. We then tried to arrange a tour in Japan; but this also fell victim to problems of financing and schedules. Ironically, the forces of change that had helped launch Crossroads now blocked our efforts to bring the message of joint Beringian heritage to both sides.

By this time it became clear that the big Crossroads which, with its large number of artifacts, heavy display cases, and complicated travel and conservation requirements, could never meet another one of our goals—that of bringing early Beringian collections back to the Native communities where they had originated. For this a new and simpler arrangement had to be made. It also seemed best to prepare a completely different exhibit, one that built upon the Crossroads themes but used artifacts from local Siberian and Alaskan museums and depended on local curators. In short we wanted to create a show that would enhance local artistic and educational programs rather than be seen as another "outsider" view of Native cultures.

With this goal in mind we assembled a team of "mini-crossroads" curators that included the project directors, Valérie Chaussonnet and William Fitzhugh, together with E. James Dixon, Richard Jordan, and Roger Powers of the University of Alaska, and Darlene Orr of the Carrie McLaine Museum in Nome. With funds from the Smithsonian and the Alaska Humanities Council, we travelled to the Russian Far East in March 1991, to inspect collections and consult with curators from museums of the Russian Far East. Staging our own "crossroads of curators," we arrived in Provideniia on a Bering Air flight from Nome and began the process of inspecting collections and discussing the possibilities of our new exhibit and cultural exchange plan.

The Russian Far East research tour, which was arranged by Valerii Shubin of the Sakhalin Museum, was wildly successful. Over a period of two weeks we were able to visit museums in Provideniia, Anadyr, Magadan, Khabarovsk, Iuzhno-Sakhalinsk, Vladivostok, and Novosibirsk, where we consulted with scientists and curators; studied collections; and made preliminary selections of exhibition materials. We returned with ideas and encouragement from new-found Russian colleagues, and during the next two years developed an exhibition plan that eventually won financial support from the Informal Science Education Program of the National Science Foundation for *Crossroads Alaska/Siberia*. The Foundation, and later the National Endowment for the Humanities, was particularly interested in using the exhibit as a pilot project for rural delivery of science and arts education.[2]

This exhibition and book, both beautifully presented by Curator Valérie Chaussonnet, are unique in several respects. While illustrating themes previously explored in the larger exhibition (cultural diversity and complexity; history, art, technology, and religion; and shared traditions and cultural patterns), "mini-Crossroads" carries these ideas directly to the peoples whoare responsible for them, in the form of a small touring exhibit and catalogue that represents the efforts and ideas of local culture experts and museum curators who represent the cultures of the North Pacific and Beringian region directly. Almost all the objects illustrated have never been published or previously exhibited. It also takes advantage of a special artistic feature of the cultures of the region—the production of detailed, elegant miniatures and models that were made specifically by their Native creators to represent these items to their own people (often, but not exclusively, to children), as well as to outsiders. By selecting miniatures and models we also solved the thorny problem of how to illustrate objects from the many cultures of the region in a small space, and, in the case of this publication, in a small book.

The presentation that follows, like the exhibit, is organized along thematic lines. Following introductions to the individual cultures that occupy the region, and their histories from ancient times to the present, the materials have been grouped into categories of subsistence, technology, domestic and social life, art, and religion. The focus throughout is on traditional cultures as they existed in the 19th-early 20th centuries, before Russian/Soviet or Euro-American cultures produced massive changes in the lives and material culture of North Pacific peoples. We have also tried to present both the traditional ethnographic views of these diverse cultures together with modern views written by contemporary cultural leaders.[3]

This exhibit and catalogue should therefore be seen in at least two dimensions. Above all, it illustrates the marvelous diversity and ingenuity of the cultures and peoples of the North Pacific region who have learned to adapt to their environments in unique and creative ways. This is especially obvious in the design of Native clothing and decorative styles applied to garments and artifacts, for which each culture has a distinctive pattern that is clearly differentiated from that of its neighbors. Second, one can see within this vast array of diversity many common themes and similarities — similarities in harpoon technology of hunting sea mammals used throughout the North Pacific coastal regions; in artifact types and ritual used by reindeer-herding peoples in Siberia; in cross-cultural similarities in hunting "harvest" festivals, in attitudes toward the dead; and in beliefs about spirits and humans' place in the world around them, and many others.

We have always thought that *Crossroads* should be seen as a beginning rather than an end. If so, we would be gratified if *Crossroads Alaska/Siberia* may at least be "the end of the beginning": the end of our effort to bring portions of the great museum collections from the North Pacific out of the storerooms and in front of the public in a way that explores diversity while at the same time seeks continuities. We also hope it is the end of a tradition in which Westerners take the lead in presenting the cultures of North Pacific peoples to others and themselves. Even in the course of our project we have seen evolution in attitudes and approaches that bring Native peoples of today into closer contact with traditional knowledge that they have been deprived of for more than 150 years. Fortunately, now there are few physical barriers to the exchange of information and materials across Bering Strait. We may hope that our experience of the 20th century will be seen as anomalous in the larger frame of time, and that the process of exchange, once reborn, will accelerate. We can only hope that the beauty of these materials will continue to inspire new generations of North Pacific peoples to express their views of themselves and the world around them with the grace and artistry seen in the creations of their ancestors. This, surely, is a proper role for museum treasures.

1
The Jesup North Pacific Expedition, directed by Franz Boas, the "father" of American Anthropology, was the first truly scientific exploration of the cultures and history of the North Pacific and took place in 1897-1903.

2
Important contributions were also made to the project by the Smithsonian's Special Exhibition Fund, the Alaska Humanities Council, the National Park Service, and the State Department's Man and the Biosphere Program.

3
Unfortunately, because of communication difficulties and printing deadlines, it was not possible to acquire contributions from Native scholars and cultural specialists from the Russian side of the Alaska-Siberia "Crossroads" area. In a future edition we hope to be able to include their perspectives on their own cultures, when the exhibit tours the Russian Far East in 1996-97. For this volume, we invited one of the leading Russian ethnographers of the region, Igor Krupnik, to present general profiles of these Siberian Native groups.

1.

First glance at the ground glass." Tanana, Alaska. F. B. Drane Collection, about 1920. University of Alaska, Fairbanks, Alaska and Polar Region Archives, neg. #91-046-520.

Introduction

Valérie Chaussonnet

"**D**welling is the manner in which mortals are on the earth." "Building Dwelling Thinking" in *Basic Writings*, Martin Heidegger

Making a dwelling a home by conceiving, fabricating, and using unique, personal, functional, or surprising objects is a universal human endeavor that found a high expression among the Native peoples of Alaska and the Russian Far East. *Crossroads Alaska* is about the living spirit of North Pacific cultures, as contained within a collection of some three hundred very old to brand new small objects. Ranging from thousand-year-old insect-shaped harpoon heads to late nineteenth-century tool boxes in the form of fish, these objects were designed to make their owner feel at home in his or her universe. Most of these artifacts were built for use in the village or away on the hunt rather than for market, and several are miniatures used as teaching aids. They were all chosen from American and Russian museum collections as objects that best tell the story of the inexhaustible creativity and resourcefulness of Alaskan and Siberian people when it comes to making the world a warmer, more beautiful, more significant, more efficient, and therefore more human home.

Dwelling is basically the art of creating one's surroundings from the existing environment and resources, according to the aesthetic and social rules of one's group. Within this context, artists have individual freedom to interpret the rules, limited only by skills or tools. North Pacific resources in terms of materials and cultural imagery are extremely vast and varied, and many artifacts presented in this exhibition testify to the joy, humor, fear, or obsessions of generations of highly skilled craftsmen and craftswomen. Unfortunately, most creators

of objects in the ethnological collections of museums are anonymous, but their heirs (the museum public and researchers, including today's Native descendants) may catch a glimpse of their minds, lives, values, and through these, of the life of a particular culture at a particular time. The artifacts in the collection presented here sometimes carry the marks of owners, users, collectors, or dealers as well. We further hope the photos in this catalogue will convey the excitement and happiness we felt in exhuming artifacts from drawers, sorting and sharing them through an exhibition.

Some pieces already travelled in previous exhibitions. These museum "stars" include the whale labret (Fig. 100), the night and day mask (Fig. 79), and some of the archeological Kodiak and Ushki pieces (Figs. 20, 21, 38, 73 and 74). Others have never been exhibited before, despite their obvious appeal (e.g. the giant goose, Fig. 49). Many were travellers before they were captured into a museum collection, many for long distances, such as every single bead in the exhibition and most of the metal. Some pieces presented here are rare, such as the Kerek dogs (Fig. 95) or the Asian Eskimo masks (Fig. 70) from the Vladivostok collections.

Crossroads Alaska has a life and character of its own. The feel of the show is intimate and precious. Because of the small size of the artifacts, one must draw close to the artifacts, as to a jewelry display.

Images are always a reduction. This catalogue is an image of an exhibition, and the exhibition an image of North Pacific cultures. However, cultures are complex. No matter how large or comprehensive the exhibition, making an exhibit about cultures is truly a magic trick! In such exhibitions, what we take to be a picture of a culture is usually what artists, the artifacts' makers, lead us to see. The hallmark of this particular exhibition is the small size of the objects, many of them miniatures and models. Indeed, *Crossroads Alaska's* miniatures are objects that were originally designed to educate, testify, and demonstrate in their Native context. Since the reduction was original and intended by the creators of the objects, we feel that through our selection we have been as loyal to the spirit of the cultures as an exhibition can be. Here these miniature teachers continue to fulfill the purpose for which they were created.

It should be obvious to all that every object has a spirit. This fact, if recognized, presents museums with a major dilemma. How can an exhibition convey the spirit of a culture through the spirit of its objects? Objects of the real world roam free and travel along nomadic paths of hunters, giftgivers, and traders long before they are trapped into storage spaces, and then sent to travel in climatically conditioned plexiglas exhibit cases. In their free state, they usually travel by pockets, small pouches, canoes, dog or reindeer sleds, and as a rule, the small ones travel the most. With *Crossroads Alaska* we have tried to return some of these small treasures to the familiar trails. We hope we have contributed at least a little to awakening among viewers some echo of the strength that created these pieces.

Inupiaq

Jana Harcharek and
Rachel Craig

2.

Barrow women sewing bearded seal skin cover over umiak frame. Photo Charles Brower. Denver Museum of Natural History, neg. #BA21-753.

Rachel Craig: Our name for ourselves is Inupiaq ("the real people"). The root of the word is *inuk* ("a person, a human being").

Jana Harcharek: I am an Inupiaq of Alaska's North Slope Borough. As the indigenous people of that region, we have occupied an area encompassing more than 90,000 square miles and sustained ourselves on its abundant natural resources for thousands of years. Archeological evidence shows that the Point Hope area has been continuously inhabited since approximately 400 B.C., though humans may have used the general area several thousand years earlier. People bearing an Inupiaq technology were using local resources in the north Alaskan interior from about A.D. 1000 until well after A.D. 1300. Inupiat continue to occupy the same area and utilize the same resources as they did centuries ago, living in harmony with one another, revering the land, the ocean, and all of its bounties.

RC: I am an Inupiaq of the NANA (Northwest Arctic Native Association) region, which lies south of the North Slope. It is a varied environment, with forests, tundra, canyons, mountains, wide valleys, sand dunes, rocky beaches, and sandy beaches. Some of its people live on the coast of Kotzebue Sound; some along the river systems. All speak Inupiaq, with varying dialects that reveal one's place of origin.

JH: Long before contact with explorers and whalers in the mid-to-late 1800s, coastal Inupiaq life was woven into a complex society based on subsistence hunting of bowhead whales (*Baleana mysticetus*). Ceremonies associated with the bowhead were practiced through-

out the year to ensure a successful season. A remarkable ceremonial building excavated at Utqiagvik, near Barrow, suggests that for prehistoric villagers, whales were the focus of social and spiritual life.

Traditional knowledge, passed from generation to generation, proves that the Inupiat had detailed information about bowhead behavior, which only recently, and only to a limited extent, has been acknowledged by western science. This knowledge endures through the continuing practice of customs associated with a subsistence lifestyle.

RC: The elders of the coastal region view Kotzebue Sound as their food-storage area. From it they harvest beluga whale, bearded seals, ringed seals, spotted seals, and walrus—not to mention salmon, humpies, trout, white fish, sheefish, herring, smelts, tomcod, flounder, and bullhead in season. In the fall, when heavy storms begin to move in before freeze-up, they harvest blue mussels along the beach and catch sea ribbons in nets.

RC: Let me tell you about the NANA region. At the west end, below the Arctic Circle, are the people of Deering, known as Ipnatchiagmiut ("people of the bluffs"). Theirs is a coastal culture. In addition to harvesting from Kotzebue Sound, they also pick berries, sourdocks, and willow leaves to vary their diet.

About 1915, teachers from the Bureau of Indian Affairs (BIA) persuaded the Natives of Deering to move their village to Putu, which was well forested and had rivers abundant with fish. However, some stayed behind and others moved in, so that today Deering is growing in popula-tion like any of our other villages. The

name of the new village was anglicized from the Inupiaq word *nuurvik* to Noorvik ("the place that people moved to"). Those of us with roots in the Deering area also have relatives in Noorvik.

The next village east is Buckland, whose people have been known as Kangigmiut since time immemorial. For centuries the Kangigmiut have harvested beluga from Escholtz Bay. This is usually a community effort right after ice break-up, the only time that the beluga migrate through that area. The Kangigmiut were also known in traditional times for their clay pottery, much sought after before metal pots and pans were brought to the region. Another delicacy from Buckland is smelts, which villagers dry every spring (now they also store them in freezers). Although Buckland people are considered coastal, they live upriver along the Buckland River.

Not far from Buckland is the ghost town of Candle. A thriving gold-mining town in the early 1900s, it had a hospital, three hotels, restaurants, and people of many ethnic groups, including Inupiat from around the region. But when the price of gold dipped, people moved away. The Kialukiigmiut are gone, but those who once lived there still return to fish or pick berries. There is also a reindeer herd at Candle.

In the east, inland, the Kuuvagmiut ("people of the big river") lived in a forested area along the Kobuk River. The Inupiaq name usually refers to people living on the Upper Kobuk in the villages of Kobuk, Shungnak, and Ambler. Being inland, the area is subject to extreme heat in summer and cold in winter. Vegetation is lush, and wild game and fish abound. In traditional times, the Kuuvagmiut's trading items were dried fish, furs, and birchbark baskets. They hunted caribou in the Noatak Mountains, using log floats to bring dried meat, fat, marrow, and skins back to the villages.

The ancient Kobuk people lived in small settlements near the headwaters of the Kuuvak, until gold miners came (1898) and schools began to be established (1905-15). Because of flooding in the spring ice break-up, some families left Kobuk to establish the village of Shungnak in the 1920s. In the 1950s, some of the Shungnak people decided to establish another village closer to sources of wild game, fish, berries, and greens. And so the town of Ambler was born.

In the delta of the Kobuk River, the people are called Kuugmiut. They have a legend that after the Great Flood covered the area, some sea serpents became land-locked. So the sea serpents dug their way out to the sea, and that's why the Kobuk River has so many bends. From the village of Kiana on down, the serpents gave birth to their young, who dug out the sloughs and smaller creeks—and that's how the Kobuk Delta was made. I like this story better than the one that scientists tell about ice ages and the receding icepack.

The village of Kiana has been there since traditional times and is known as Katyaak ("the fork where the rivers meet"). Many families take pride in tracing their roots to Katyaak. The Gold Rush rejuvenated the site, and the English language made a big impact on the culture. However, subsistence food gathering still continues here, as it does in all of our villages.

Downstream from Kiana is Noorvik (mentioned above), established around 1915. A thriving community of coastal and river people, today it is one of the largest villages in the region. Noorvik once had a sawmill and a hospital, but now the sawmill is abandoned and the old hospital has become living quarters for teachers.

In the northern part of the NANA region, just south of the North Slope, is Kivalina, originally a summer campsite along the Singaq, a favorite site for seal hunting, fishing, and berry picking. One summer, BIA teachers proceeded to build a school there. In the meantime, the Native people went back upriver to their winter homes, close to supplies of wood for heating, cooking, and building. Soon, however, they found they had to move back to Kivalina if they had children of school age. Living on the coast was difficult, far from wood and favorite fishing areas, but the BIA teachers had the power to make them conform. Today, the village of Kivalina is considering a move to higher ground. With global warming, the water table is rising, the beach on the ocean side is shrinking, and the land on the

lagoon side is eroding. There is no room for new houses and families crowd into existing homes. So much for decisions by government people with no experience in the Arctic!

Southeast of Kivalina is Noatak, where two groups of people lived. Those who settled in the forest were the Napaaqtugmiut ("people of the forest"). The other group, the Nunataagmiut, traveled to the headwaters of the Noatak River every year, following the caribou. After ice break-up in the spring, they returned to the coast to fish, hunt sea mammals, and pick berries. In between many of these villages are hunting camps.

In the center of the NANA region, on the coast, is the village of Kotzebue, named for Otto von Kotzebue, a Russian explorer of German origin. But from time immemorial, the village has been called Qiqiqtagruk ("the big island"). Qiqiqtagruk has always been the hub of the region. Before any stores were built, huge trade fairs were held here, with people from the interior and from the coast briskly trading with each other. Some Eskimos even came over from Siberia with tobacco and reindeer skins to trade. Old Eskimos talk of previous generations crawling into bed to sleep off the effects of Siberian tobacco. It may have been mixed with opium.

JH: On the North Slope, the arrival of missionaries and institutionalized "education," beginning about 1900, has had its consequences. Churches nearly eradicated traditional religiou. Shamanistic rituals are no longer practiced, although some elders have information about these rites. Fortunately, song and dance have remained strong. The recent revival of Kivgiq ("messenger feast") means that people have retained intricate ceremonial dance forms through the ages.

RC: The education system almost totally destroyed our traditional culture. Because our parents were punished in school for speaking Inupiaq, they tried to make school easier for us by speaking only English to us. In this way they inadvertently became an extension of BIA teachers who wanted to make us assimilate into industrial society.

Since then, however, we have developed an Inupiaq language curriculum and are teaching it in school. But to be successful, this effort must have the support of Inupiaq speakers at home. Few parents speak the language now; for some students, Inupiaq has become a secret language that their parents can't understand.

JH: Traditionally, education consisted in acquiring survival skills. One learned how to navigate on sea and land, in all weathers, using astronomy, wind, ocean currents, weather

patterns, and land forms. Skill in hunting was and still is necessary for cultural continuity in the Arctic.

Modernization has meant that people must be equipped both with traditional skills, which enable them to thrive culturally, and with skills needed for success in the modern world. Inupiat had to institute forms of government and corporate enterprise that were initially foreign to them; they must now have formal schooling in order to profit from these opportunities. But their experience of survival in the Arctic has taught them how to adapt to their environment and rise to challenges.

RC: Our region is much like other rural areas of Alaska. We have worked hard to get decent housing, water, sewers, telecommunications, health services, education, and job opportunities for our villages. We have developed a world-class mine in partnership with Canadians, but with metal prices very low, we don't know how long the mine will stay open. We still need to develop activities for youth, to keep them from the alcohol and drug culture. We also want to instill in them our traditional values, our hunting skills, our survival techniques, and to ground them in their identity as Inupiaq people.

JH: The Alaska Native Claims Settlement Act of 1971 mandated the formation of regional and village corporations. In response, the Inupiat formed the Arctic Slope Regional Corporation and various village corporations. In addition, the North Slope Borough was incorporated as a home-rule government in 1972. Its primary goal was to provide residents with the same basic services enjoyed by other Americans. Since then, schools, clinics, fire stations, housing, and other service facilities have been built. The regional and village corporations have prospered. Many young Inupiat attend prestigious schools and colleges to learn how successful corporations are run and how governments can benefit people.

RC: Whatever happens, we are very much concerned that our people continue to provide for their families through subsistence hunting, fishing, and plant-gathering. There is not enough local industry to replace our subsistence activities. That is how our forefathers lived; it is the way we live.

JH: Many challenges face the Inupiat today. In addition to having to adapt to changes caused by development, we also need to maintain those values that make us who we are. This means taking the best of what both worlds have to offer and remembering always those values taught us by our ancestors.

For further reading, see: Burch 1984; Hall 1984; and Spencer 1984.

Yupik

Larry Kairaiuak and
Darlene Orr

3.

Yupik couple sewing skins and using a bow drill inside tent. Skinner Foundation Collection. Alaska State Library, neg. #PCA 44-11-1.

Larry Kairaiuak: The *Yupiit* ("the real people") of the Yukon-Kuskokwim River delta were one of the last Native peoples to be invaded by outsiders. There has not been much contact, due to the lack of natural resources in the region, so Yupik Eskimos have maintained most of their traditions, culture, and language.

Yupik communities cover a large area of western Alaska, chiefly along rivers and the Bering Sea coast. Many Yupik villages consist of several large extended families. As in most Native communities in Alaska, this social structure has produced a tradition of sharing and giving.

Darlene Orr: As a Siberian Yupik growing up on St. Lawrence Island in the Bering Sea, I heard stories of the *Ungazighmiit*, the other Siberian Yupik people who lived in the forbidding Soviet Union. But nothing that I heard prepared me for my first meeting with one. For forty years the Cold War had cut off all communication and travel in the Bering Strait region. Before then, since time immemorial, the Siberian Yupik had moved freely and frequently between St. Lawrence Island and the coast of Chukotka in Russia, a distance of only 40 miles. When the "Ice Curtain" came down, the two halves of the Yupik population were cut off from each other, but the mountainous Soviet coast constantly reminded St. Lawrence Islanders that there were friends and kin on the other side.

It wasn't until 1988 that we began to rediscover those ties, when the Soviet government allowed a "Friendship Flight" from Alaska to the port town of Provideniia in Chukotka. I was among the twenty Yupik passengers on that flight. Shortly after I stepped off the plane, a Native man came up to me and said in Yupik, "I'm from the Kivak clan. Which clan are you from?" I was speechless. Here was a man from a different country, speaking my Native language, telling me he was from the same clan I was!

That trip was the first of many exchanges between the two sides. Today, Yupik people can travel back and forth without visas.

LK: The indigenous people of Alaska believe that there was a time when people could become animals, and animals could become people. A special relationship linked people to animals, the spirit world, land, and sea. This unique connection to the universe has been essential to survival in the arctic regions. In the animal world, the members of each species look after each other. They warn each other when danger is near, or they call others when one finds food or a safe haven. They bring food for their young that are not capable of surviving on their own.

DO: On the American side, most Yupik people live on St. Lawrence Island, 200 miles off the Alaskan coast and 40 miles from the Russian mainland. Two villages are on the island, Savoonga and Gambell, each with a population of 550. In Chukotka, the communities with dominant Yupik populations are Sireniki and New Chaplino. Sireniki has a population of 800, of which a little more than half are Yupik; in New Chaplino most of the 500 residents are Yupik. New Chaplino used to be the tradi-

tional coastal village of Ungaziq (Chaplino), but in 1958 the Soviet government saw fit to move it inland. The Russian Yupik were made to live within fluctuating boundaries shared by Russians and Chukchi. The Chukchi and Russian people have become the majority in an area that was once occupied by Yupik alone.

Forced relocations and the presence of other cultures have had an adverse effect on the Yupik (Chaplinski) language. Today virtually no one under the age of 30 speaks Chaplinski. Although literacy in the Native language began in 1932, it was subject to many changes under Soviet policies. Chaplinski was used to teach Russian and to disseminate Communist beliefs. The younger generation of Chaplinski speakers has been affected by Russian pronunciation. Of course, they say we're the ones who have the strange accent.

Unlike Chukotka, few people on St. Lawrence Island are non-Yupik, and most islanders still speak Siberian Yupik. However, with the introduction of television, VCRs, and radio, English is quickly becoming a major force of change in language and culture.

LK: When a Yupik hunter catches game of any kind, he distributes it to relatives or other community members. Elders, widows, and families who are unable to provide for themselves are the first to receive a share. There are also other kinds of sharing rituals. Every spring, a seal party is given in honor of the first bearded seal caught that season, or the first game caught by a young hunter. Food, clothing, and toys are given away at the seal party.

Another custom is being revived in south-western Yupik communities. Residents of a community prepare for this event for months, and invite several surrounding communities, the extended relatives of the host village. This event lasts for several days. Traditional Eskimo dancing takes place every night, and each village takes turns in providing the entertainment. The host village entertains on the final night, and gifts are distributed to guests that night or the following day. Gifts range from local foods that were collected during the year, to clothing or store-bought items. Community members' accomplishments are recognized at this time as well. If a child has gathered berries for the first time, the parents or grandparents give plastic bags of frozen berries to elders from the invited villages or to relatives of the deceased person for whom the child is named.

DO: Another aspect of Yupik life that differs on both sides is the economic base. On St. Lawrence Island, Yupik still practice subsistence hunting and fishing, with much the same traditional patterns of distribution. Technologically, American hunters are more advanced than their Russian counterparts, having the latest models of boats, outboard motors, snow machines, and all-terrain vehicles available to them. On the Russian side, equipment is often antiquated or homemade. Under the Soviet system, all equipment belonged to collective and state farms. On these cooperatives, chosen members of a community have the jobs of hunting, fishing, trapping, and fur farming. They are paid in cash and in kind.

LK: Our villages maintain a subsistence lifestyle, and our survival is tied to the land and sea. A respect for all things in the Yupik environment, sometimes a harsh and unpredictable one, is basic to survival. Yupik always treat the animals they catch with respect. This tradition of handling game respectfully, from the moment it is caught until it is consumed, has been passed on from one generation to another. Our thoughts and actions affect the success of each hunt or gathering of wild plants.

Yupik believe that animals give themselves up for us to eat, therefore we must pay respect to them as well as the environment that provides these animals.

DO: With the collapse of Communism, life in the former Soviet Union has been changing at a breathtaking pace. While good things can be said for its demise, the totalitarian system actually helped to maintain one aspect of Yupik culture: spiritual beliefs. On St. Lawrence Island, the first missionaries arrived in 1894, exerting their influence to replace the Native religion with Christianity. They succeeded. On the Soviet side, Yupik retained more of their Native beliefs because Communism proved to be an inadequate replacement. Spiritual beliefs were also reinforced by old Russian customs.

LK: Among the Yupik, Ellam Yua (Spirit of the Universe), the equivalent of the Christian God, was the basis of all spirituality. Ellam Yua provided and watched over everything in existence. Today, Yupik still speak about Ellam Yua, regardless of the dominant religions in the region—the Moravian, Russian Orthodox, and Catholic churches.

DO: Recently in Provideniia, visiting the family of a deceased friend, I brought Native food with me. The family put some food aside to be placed in a fire so that the spirit could partake of it. Another practice I observed was the placing of a pot in the middle of the deceased person's living room to keep evil spirits at bay.

Traditional spiritual customs are still observed on the Russian side, where Christianity hasn't had much influence. Such traditional practices have ceased on St. Lawrence Island. With the increased travel to Russia now, missionaries have been bringing their Christian message to the Yupik villages, and it has had a warm reception from some people. At present, with a depressed Russian economy and low morale, almost anything from America is seen as wonderful.

LK: Death within a community allows people to give and share. When someone dies, relatives and friends look after the family. The community grieves together. People from surrounding villages also take part in this event. After the funeral, family and relatives host a potlatch for the village and visitors from nearby villages.

One way of easing the pain of loss of a loved one is to name a child after the deceased. The child is often spoken to or treated in exactly the same way as the person for whom he or she is named. Relatives of the deceased give the child gifts of all kinds, ranging from the deceased's favorite foods to clothing or toys at special occasions. Yupik believe that no one really passes out of existence, and that when a child is named after a deceased person, that person's soul is reborn. In one case, a child was named after his paternal grandfather, who had died about four years before. Because a girl child in the family had already been given the grandfather's name, some people in the village would not address the boy by name, insisting that the older child had the name first. One woman was adamant until she dreamed that the deceased grandfather was making tea by squeezing used tea bags. The next morning, she visited the boy's mother and asked if any of her children made tea that way.

The mother replied that her son did. The woman told the mother about her dream and asked her to give the boy a fresh cup of tea from now on. From that time, the woman addressed the boy by the grandfather's name.

DO: Under Soviet rule, traditional ivory/bone carving and Native dancing was transformed into an economic resource. Carvers work in a cooperative where they perfect their craft under a master (often a Chukchi), and dancers perform as a professional ensemble. Compared to Yupik dancers from St. Lawrence Island, Russian Yupik dancers look very dramatic and polished. But most people don't realize that they are trained to be professional dancers. On St. Lawrence Island, anybody can dance if they want, as it is a form of recreation and not livelihood.

Carving on the island is still done on individual basis, too, as a means of bringing in cash. A controversial source of cash is the selling of ancient artifacts dug up at traditional village sites around the island. This method of getting quick money now holds an attraction to Yupik on the Russian side. This is especially true since the country's economy has been in upheaval, and any means of extra income appears good.

Life for American Yupik is better in terms of access to material goods, but that does not necessarily guarantee a higher quality of life. In fact, many people on St. Lawrence Island are on some form of government assistance. (Russian Yupik also received government assistance, but were required to hold a job in return.) Unfortunately, St. Lawrence Islanders share with the Russian Yupik the problems of alcoholism, suicide, and violence. However, with the opening of the border and the renewal of kinship ties, a sense of pride is being re-established among the Yupik people. The younger generation of Russian Yupik is now making an attempt to speak their Native language again, and there is great interest in cultural exchanges on both sides. We see changes from the reunification of this culture, and we also see the effects from forty years of separation and acculturation, yet we can only guess what the future holds for the once homogenous Siberian Yupik people.

For further reading, see: Damas 1984; Fienup-Riordan 1983, 1990; Fitzhugh and Kaplan 1982; and Yugtun Qaneryaramek Calivik n.d.

Alutiiq

Gordon L. Pullar and
Richard A. Knecht

4.

A procession of villagers escorts Bishop Gregory Afonsky to church for a service celebrating his arrival in Tatitlek. Photo Eric Hill, Anchorage Daily News, 1989.

As the decade of the 1990s opened, the Alutiiq people of south-central Alaska were singing and performing traditional dances, carving ceremonial masks, making traditional clothing, building kayaks, and taking action to preserve their language. Only a decade before, many thought that these symbols of Alutiiq culture had perhaps vanished forever. Then the Kodiak Area Native Association (KANA), the regional tribal organization of the Alutiiq of Kodiak Island, began efforts to preserve and revitalize traditional culture. This movement spread to the Alutiiq people of Prince William Sound and the Kenai and Alaska peninsulas. Associated with this effort has been a "sobriety movement" that addresses the issue of alcohol abuse at a grassroots level, as well as new efforts of taking control of political power and resource management. Several Alutiiq communities have implemented mariculture and salmon hatchery programs to develop an economic base. The

Kodiak Island village of Larsen Bay secured the repatriation of nearly 800 human skeletons excavated in the village in the 1930s and shipped to the Smithsonian Institution. An elaborate reburial ceremony took place in 1991. Now Prince William Sound Alutiiq communities are in the process of repatriating human remains taken from that area. Today Alutiiq communities are expe-riencing a significant resurgence of pride in their heritage and ethnic identity.

History

The struggle for the survival of Alutiiq culture came in the wake of 250 years of acculturation, first to Russian culture and then, beginning in 1867, to American culture. This intense period of contact followed more than 7,000 years of flourishing culture and population growth. The first European landing in Alaska, by Danish explorer Vitus Bering in 1741 on behalf of Russia, was on Kayak Island in Prince William Sound, in northern Alutiiq territory. Ships bearing Russian fur hunters began to contact Alutiiq people regularly by the 1760s. Alutiiq culture was at its peak at

that time, with an estimated population of 20,000 spread among numerous villages, some with as many as 1,000 inhabitants (Jordan and Knecht 1988:232; Crowell 1988:132-135; Hrdlicka 1944:19).

The Alutiiq fiercely resisted the Russian presence; mass attacks by armored Alutiiq warriors were repelled only by firearms, which were unfamiliar and frightening to people in a land where thunder is rarely heard. For two decades, they withstood Russian attempts to occupy Kodiak Island (Black 1990). Finally the Siberian merchant Gregori Shelikhov loaded two ships with men, muskets, and cannon and arrived at Three Saints Bay in August 1784. He demanded that ruling families among the Alutiiq provide their children as hostages. Terrified villagers gathered children, elders, and warriors—as many as 2,000 in all— on a fortified sea stack (a column of rock rising out of the sea). Alutiiq people had long used such refuges when attacked by invaders.

Shelikhov attacked in the early morning hours of August 13, 1784. Five small cannons panicked the Alutiiq defenders, and seventy-one Russians stormed up the cliffs. In the ensuing pandemonium, many hundreds died. Male adults and elders were executed—hundreds, according to some Russian accounts. About 500 women and children were taken to Three Saints Bay as hostages. Alaska became Russian, and Alutiiq life changed forever. The Alutiiq name for the rock is A'wauq, which means "to become numb" (Knecht, Haakanson, and Dickson n.d.)

Alutiiq people soon became impressed laborers for the Russian-American Company. Hunters were forced to join in the hunt for sea otters. Women were set to sew clothing, gather berries, and perform other tasks. Even the aged were put to work gathering bird eggs from the sea cliffs. Epidemics of disease hitherto unknown among the people devastated entire villages (Fortuine 1989:201). Elders, the vital tradition-bearers in a culture without a written language, were among the first to die. Family trees, epic stories, songs, and specialized knowledge, accumulated through thousands of years, died with the elders. In the villages, even today, the death of a elder is like a library burning. Eventually the Russian Orthodox Church intervened, and the company began to relax its grip. By the mid-1800s, the population on Kodiak Island had dropped from 10,000 to about 1,500 (Holmberg 1985:36).

In 1867 Alutiiq lives were again jolted when the Americans occupied Alaska. Canneries sprang up near many villages, and thousands of workers poured into the area. Salmon, the staple of the Alutiiq diet, became a commercial commodity and fed the American economy thousands of miles away. Over-fishing wiped out runs of salmon that had fed Natives for many generations. Lines appeared on the map as land also became a thing to be owned. Alcohol became yet another epidemic that brought death and loss, as it does today. Traditional clothing and housing, tolerated and even adopted by the Russians, were viewed as backward by the Americans, and soon began to disappear.

Schools and missions brought more unfamiliar ways and a new language. Teachers punished children for speaking the Alutiiq language, a practice that persisted into the 1960s. The kayak, which held a place for the Alutiiq as the horse did for the Plains Indian, was discarded in favor of wooden skiffs. The sea otter hunt also became a thing of memory, as sea otters were nearly extinct by the early 1900s. World War II wroughtstill more changes to the Alutiiq people. Roads and airstrips brought strangers into towns and villages that had been reachable only by sea. More young people traveled outside Alaska, usually for the first time; some returned, but as changed people.

Over the past three decades, two major disasters struck Alutiiq communities. The first was the Great Alaska Earthquake of 1964, which destroyed several Alutiiq villages. The second disaster fell on March 24, 1989, when the oil tanker *Exxon Valdez* ran aground in Prince William Sound, just four miles from the Alutiiq village of Tatilek. Eleven million gallons of crude oil spread through the sound, affecting all the Alutiiq villages. While the long-term effect of the spill is being debated, the trauma it has caused remains evident.

Alutiiq Identity

The identity of the Alutiiq people is often confusing to many. Russian fur traders in the 18th and 19th centuries applied the term Aleut to both the indigenous people of the Aleutian Islands (who called themselves Unangan) and to the Alutiiq (who called themselves Sugpiaq) (Clark 1984:195-196). These two cultures have many differences, however, including different languages. The Alutiiq language was known as Sugcestun or Suk.

The Alutiiq people include at least three major subgroups: the Chugachmiut of Prince William Sound, the Unegkurmiut of the Kenai Peninsula, and the Qikertarmiut of Kodiak Island. The Alutiiq are also sometimes called Koniagmiut or Koniag. Because of close linguistic relationship with the Inuit people of the Arctic, anthropologists have often classified the Alutiiq as Eskimos—a label that the Alutiiq strenuously object to.

Alutiiq Political Structures

Once, each Alutiiq village was governed by a chief (*Toyuq*), a second chief (*Sukashiq*), a third chief (*Staristaq*) who was the lay reader of the village's Russian Orthodox Church, and a council of elders (KANA 1987:1). Elders today still speak of the old tribal governments and their effectiveness.

By the 1970s new political systems were in place in Alutiiq communities. The federal Bureau of Indian Affairs required a model of tribal government that fit its own needs rather than those of the communities. Some villages formed governments under the federal Indian Reorganization Act. Others set up an elected council headed by a "president" (these are called "traditional councils" although they are modeled after the U.S. government rather than a traditional system).

Although not officially political bodies, the corporations formed under the Alaska Native Claims Settlement Act (ANCSA) of 1971 exert considerable political influence in managing land and other resources. ANCSA's intention was to divide the state along cultural boundaries, with each major Native group creating a regional "for-profit" corporation. The Alutiiq cultural area, however, was divided in three sections. Thus the Alutiiq of Kodiak Island are represented by Koniag, Inc.; Prince William Sound and the Kenai Peninsula are represented by the Chugach Alaska Corporation; and Alaska Peninsula by the Bristol Bay Native Corporation. This has created new issues of identity, as many Alutiiq people—like other Native groups in Alaska—tend to identify themselves first as shareholders in a particular regional corporation rather than an ethnic identity.

The Alutiiq tribal governments of today have also utilized the geographic boundaries established by ANCSA to create regional tribal organizations that provide health, social, educational, and cultural programs to the villages and represent the villages in political issues. These organizations are the Kodiak Area Native Association, Chugachmiut, and the Bristol Bay Native Association.

Conclusion

The people of the twenty remaining Alutiiq communities are addressing the impact of the past 250 years of contact. There is little doubt that the catastrophic events of that period have had a cumulative effect on today's Alutiiq people and their culture. Today, however, the resurgence of cultural pride and ethnic identity, control of resources, and political power is reshaping the future for Alutiiq people and their communities. They have weathered the latest storms and will decide what they will allow to be changed in their culture and what they will retain. They control their own destiny.

"Our people have made it through lots of storms and disasters for thousands of years. All the troubles since the Russians are like one long stretch of bad weather. Like everything else, this storm will pass over some day."

—Barbara Shangin, Alutiiq elder, Chignik Lake, 1987

For further reading, see: Black 1990; Clark 1984; Crowell 1988a; Davis 1984; Fortuine 1989; Holmberg 1985; Hrdlicka1944; Jordan and Knecht 1988; Knecht, Haakanson, and Dickson n.d.; Kodiak Area Native Association 1987; and Pullar 1992.

Aleut

Barbara Śvarný Carlson

5.

Aleuts on board ship at Unalaska, being relocated away from the war zone during the summer of 1942. All of the Aleuts on the Pribilof Islands and along the Aleutian chain up to Akutan were hastily removed and forced to live in extremely primitive conditions in long-abandoned canneries in southeast Alaska, where many died from ill health. They were kept there and only allowed to return at the conclusion of the war in 1945. The village of Attu was captured by the Japanese and the people sent to Japan where a third of them died. Surviving Attuans were forced to live at Atka upon their release from Japanese captivity. National Archives, neg. #80-6-12163. Courtesy of the Aleut Pribilof Association.

There is no such thing as an Aleut. We call ourselves Unangan, or Unangas in the Atkan dialect. This is our name for ourselves, the indigenous people of the Aleutian Archipelago.

When Russian explorers came to our land, the first island people that they came upon were the Sasxinan, who lived in what the Russians named the Near Islands, because they lie near Russia at the western end of the Aleutians. For uncertain reasons, the Russians called them Aleut, and as they moved eastward on their conquest, the Russians continued to call the people Aleut—even when they crossed a major dividing line of language and culture and encountered Alutiiq-speaking people (previously called Sugpiaq) of the Alaska Peninsula. Recognizing a language difference, however, they sometimes referred to us as Fox Aleuts and the Alutiiq as Koniag Aleuts. The Russian language became the common denominator of acculturation among these diverse groups.

We "Aleuts" are actually three different maritime peoples who had their own identities and subdivisions before contact: the Alutiiq-speakers, the Central Yupik-speakers of Bristol Bay, and the Unangam Tunuu-speakers. Why should we hang on to "Aleut," a foreign name? We should revive our original names to show pride in our cultural heritage and to reclaim and maintain our identities as a distinct people.

Who We Are:
Pre-Contact Tribes and Dialects

Unangax̂ is the singular form of a word whose stem, *una*, refers to the seaside. Unangan and Unangas are plural forms, and Unangam is the possessive.

Before contact, the Unangan may have had as many as nine distinct subgroups, or tribes, and dialects. Where possible, the major islands are named in the indigenous language (see Bergsland 1994 and map p. 108); foreign names are in parentheses. From west to east:

1) the Sasxinan, on: (Near Islands); Atux̂ (Attu), Samiyax̂ (Shemya), and Angatux̂ (Agattu);
2) the Qax̂un, on: (Rat Islands); Amchixtax̂ (Amchitka), Idmaax (Buldir), Qixsa (Kiska), and Unyax (Semisopochnoi);
3) the Naahmiĝus, on: (Delarof Islands); Tanax̂ax (Tanaga), and Amatignax̂ (Amatignak);
4) the Niiĝuĝis, on: (Andreanof Islands); Kanaga (Kanaga), Adaagix̂ (Adak), Atx̂ax̂ (Atka), Amlax (Amlia), and Saĝuugamax (Seguam);
5) the Akuuĝun or Uniiĝun, on: (Islands of the Four Mountains); Qagaamila (Kagamil), Amuux̂tax̂ (Amukta), Yunax̂sxa (Yunaska), and Chuginadax;
6) the Qawalangin, on: (Fox Islands); Samalĝa (Samalga), Umnax (Umnak), Nawan-Alaxsxa [one of the earliest recorded names for Unalaska], Amiq or Tanax̂-Amix̂ (St. Paul), Anĝaaxchalux̂ (St. George), Xulustaakan Tanĝingin (The Seals' Place), and (Pribilof Islands);
7) the Qigiiĝun, on: (Krenitzin Islands); Sidaanax̂ (Sedanka), Akutanax̂ (Akutan), Akungan (Akun), and Qiqalĝan (Tigalda);

8) the Qaĝaan Tayaĝungin, whose homeland extends to Port Moller on the north side of Alaska Peninsula and Kupreanof Point on the south side; Unimax (Unimak), Sanaĝax̂ (Sanak), and Quduĝin (Pavlov Island); 9) the Qaĝiiĝun, on (Shumagin Islands); Uĝnaasaqax̂ (Unga), (Nagai), (Big Koniuji), Tanĝimax (Little Koniuji), Tanĝanuk (Korovin), and Siitikdax̂ (Popof); the Qaĝiiĝun are sometimes included with Qagaan Tayaĝungin.

Traditionally, we did not live beyond Kupreanof Point on the Alaska Peninsula. We called the people who lived beyond that, Kanaaĝin.

The Sasxinan dialect is no longer spoken in this country. During World War II, the Sasxinan were wrenched from their island of Atux̂ (Attu) and taken as prisoners to Japan. After returning to this country upon liberation, the twenty-four survivors were denied repatriation to Atux̂; instead the United States government moved them to Atx̂ax̂ (Atka), the home of the Niiĝuĝis. There the Sasxinan needed to adopt the Niiĝuĝis dialect.

However, the Sasxinan language survives in Russia. In the 1830s, the Russians forcibly removed some Sasxinan from Atux̂ to the Commander Islands; a small number of their descendants still live there and speak a highly Russianized version of the Sasxinan dialect. On the other Commander Island, Bering, a few elders still speak Niiĝuĝis. In the 1960s the Russians evacuated the Sasxinan from Copper to Bering Island. The Russians had similarly transported Niiĝuĝis from Atx̂ax̂, for seasonal and permanent labor in the harvesting of fur seals, but predominantly they moved Qawalangin from Unalaska to the Pribilof Islands (Jones 1980).

The Urgent Work of Reclamation and Revitalization

It has been predicted that the Unangam language may be extinct by the year 2055. If it dies out, indigenous knowledge preserved in that language may also disappear.

Tanang awaa ("work of my country") is a formulaic beginning that opens certain storytelling sessions of the Unangan. These words announce that the information presented is proudly shared as a product of a larger body, the collective people. In our region, the work of individuals is valued, but cooperative efforts are of infinitely loftier value. In the oral tradition, stories and narratives were passed down from one generation to the next, but sometime after contact the stories ceased to be told in public places, then ceased, in most cases, to be told at all.

Much ethnographic information can be extracted from the surviving stories and narratives of the Unangan. The cooperative marriage of indigenous information with modern technology can help to retrieve indigenous information—in basketry, design, carved works, literature, medicinal plants, science, humor, subsistence, or similarly valuable things—for the benefit of all. But the survival of the Unangam way of life is paramount to this venture. If information survives without the people, then the world will have lost a crucial ingredient in the recipe for the survival of mankind and the management of renewable resources.

Our Unangam identities have become so tenuous that we are excavating, sifting, and meticulously labeling the artifacts of our society with increasing fervor. If we do not, something may disappear forever. The endangered Unangam language is a virtually untapped resource of clues about our history, found objects, our profound relationship with land and sea, rules to live by, and perhaps most importantly, a unique view of the world. The Unangam folklore is a vital part of our contribution to the world bank of knowledge.

Looking toward the Future

People who have left their Unangam villages have a deepened sense of the sacred value of their origins, as seems to be a trend among Alaska Natives. They feel a loss—be it of Native foods, songs, dance, stories, or seeing beauty reflected in artfully made objects. They miss seeing other people who look like them; they miss feeling the wind, fog, salty air, the rain that comes at you sideways. They need to know about their heritage and to share that knowledge with family and community. They need to hear someone shout, *"Aang, Unangax̂!"* (Hello, "Aleut"). Many of those people are searching for these things when they return to the village or to Alaska. These people consider their original villages home even if they have not been able to return for many years. They share a common feeling: "Where we are from is important to us. What we like to eat is important. Our art is important. Our dance and music are important."

Unangam foods are elemental to our culture. To have Native foods sent to us when we are away is one of the most vitalizing, identity-rich gifts that friends or family can bestow. Some of our traditional subsistence foods include alax̂ (whale), isux̂ (hair seal), aanux̂ (red salmon), and qax̂ (any kind of fish). From the beaches some favorites are: chiknan (limpets), waygin (blue mussels), aguĝaadan (sea urchins), qasiiqun (chitons or gumboots), chalan (clams), and kahngadgin (seaweed). Saaqudax̂ (cow parsnip, "puuchki-is" in Russian), fiddlehead ferns and other native vegetables seem to make one feel

healthier. My personal favorite is dried salmon with chadux̂ (seal oil). *Qaĝaasakung* ("thank you") to my parents, who generously keep me supplied. Without it, I would not be able to feel so strongly who I am!

There is an ambivalence I feel when I walk into a museum exhibit, touched to the core by what I see. I feel gratitude and wonder that these beautiful and precious objects have been collected and cared for so that people like myself can learn from them. I appreciate the labors of so many people—archeologists, anthropologists, educators, linguists, and others. At the same time, I grieve that many of the villages where these items came from are now virtually empty of their original cultural property.

There is a sad irony in the relations between museums and indigenous peoples. On the one hand, the collection and preservation of these artifacts is a major aid to cultural reclamation and revitalization. On the other hand, it is a tragedy that these precious remnants of our cultural heritage lie on display in lands sometimes unknown to their original owners. There is an awesome responsibility that pairs museum institutions and indigenous peoples as equal partners as we both search for culturally appropriate ways to document traditional knowledge and skills. The cooperative spirit of repatriation in evidence all over the world is an encouraging statement of humanism. This traveling exhibit, *Crossroads Alaska,* is a testament to hosts of kindred spirits who have labored to share this marvelous collection. This is one method of repatriating indigenous things: to make this fine project accessible to small Alaskan communities where the works will be studied and appreciated. These valuable links to Unangam culture are validation of our origins, touchstones to our identities.

Acknowledgments

Qaĝaasakung ("thank you") to Knut Bergsland, Professor Emeritus, University of Oslo; Moses L. Dirks; Nick Galaktionoff; Platonida Gromoff; Michael Krauss, Alaska Native Language Center, University of Alaska Fairbanks; and Doug Veltre, Department of Anthropology, University of Alaska Anchorage.

For further reading, see: Bergsland 1994; Bergsland and Dirks 1990; and Jones 1980.

Athapaskan

Melinda Chase,
Miranda Wright,
and Bernice Joseph

6.

*Athapaskan fiddler
Bill Stevens
teaches Robert John
at Ft. Yukon.
Photo James H.
Barker, 1990.*

The Athapaskan people of Alaska call themselves Den'a ("the people"). They speak eleven different languages, and the lands they call home range from south of the Brooks Range, east to the Canadian border, south to the Cook Inlet, and west as far as the Nulato Hills. This expanse of territory is covered with low hills and flat lands, broken by the Alaska Range and shaped by extensive waterways including the Tanana, Kuskokwim, and Yukon rivers.

Prior to contact, the land provided what the Den'a needed. Each regional band had its own territory, which was divided among several small localized bands consisting mainly of extended families. These bands followed established trails on their seasonal quest for food. Periodically, they would "gather-up" or assemble as a group for ceremonies throughout the year.

As dictated by past generations, the life cycle of contemporary Athapaskans continues to flow with the seasons. Fall means intensive work during the moose or caribou hunt. As the days shorten and become colder, sewing and trapping occupy the hours of Athapaskans preparing for a "give-away" ceremony. A renewal of energy is associated with spring, a time for goose and duck hunts, beaver trapping, and village carnivals highlighted with dog-sled races. Fishing, berry-picking, construction, and picnics are activities associated with summer.

A Holistic World-View

The Den'a see a unity in the human, natural, and spiritual worlds; in both the seen and unseen worlds, all things have a spirit, and everything is connected. This holistic world-view is implicitly expressed in Den'a ceremonies. It is explicitly expressed in the sharing of water and food, and often in the use of fire.

Anthropologists have classified many Den'a ceremonies, feasts, and healing rituals as "potlatches," "feasts for the dead," "mortuary feasts," or "memorial potlatches." While a potlatch is formally defined as the distribution of material wealth as a means to increase social recognition, this term is only a superficial description of a traditional ceremony, overlooking the scope, intention, and deeper meaning of many Den'a ceremonies.

Ceremonies

A brief examination of Athapaskan ceremonies will reveal the deeper meaning of Den'a rituals. Water, food, fire, song, and dance are important elements in many of these ceremonies. As the body is nourished by food and water, so is the soul fed through music and dance. Fire provides an avenue to the spiritual world. The cooperation required to conduct these ceremonies, whose great antiquity dictates protocol and procedure, makes each a community event. To the untrained observer, organization appears haphazard. However, upon closer scrutiny, the protocol established in the distant past becomes evident.

In the Athapaskan culture, when a person dies, the whole village comes together to grieve with family and friends of the deceased. After the person is laid to rest, a strong spiritual connection is maintained through water, food, song, and dance as the Den'a prepare to free the *yega* or spirit for its next journey in the Den'a life cycle.

Women share memories of the deceased as they gather to bead and to sew garments for the "give-away." Men share memories while on their hunting or fishing excursions. These are occasions for expressing grief as members tell stories, laugh, cry, and express anger, guilt, sorrow, or love.

Grief and/or guilt are also expressed through songs composed for the deceased. These eulogies immortalize the talents and works of the deceased and are an important part of community cohesiveness. In earlier times, our people took note when someone excelled in a particular area; however, this did not make him or her better than the rest, for everyone had their place in the community. A death in the community creates a void—for example, the loss of a good hunter, an understanding friend, a fast runner, an industrious worker, a loving member of a family, or a community leader. The process of composing these songs provides an avenue for healing as the absence of this family member is directly addressed. In learning to sing these songs, community members go through the same healing process as the composer.

By giving gifts to those who came together to grieve with family and friends, the family pays the earthly debts of the deceased. Once these ties to mother earth are severed, the *yega* (spirit) of the deceased is free to continue its life cycle in the next dimension. The *yega* of the animal kingdom is also honored as gifts of traditional food are placed in a fire to nourish the deceased as he or she adjusts to life in a different world. This adjustment period applies to the mourners as well. Active participation in a healing ceremony provides an avenue to deal with grief or guilt while adjusting to the void created in the community through the loss of a member. These rituals restore social balance and order to the family and to the community.

Reaffirming the community as a living entity while maintaining the health of the individual is an important feature of Den'a healing ceremonies. At a recent "memorial potlatch" in Minto, a Den'a elder thanked those in attendance for taking the time to join in their ceremony, saying "You help lift us up. We support one another. We come together to honor special people, but in the process we also honor one another and ourselves."

Conclusion

Transition from oral to written communication has brought vast changes in the way Den'a stories and histories are told. By itself, the literature offers a limited scope, perception, and understanding of Den'a belief. Repeated visits, stories, and inclusion in celebrations and healing ceremonies are needed to open the soul to a real view of the Athapaskan world. It is through participation that the significance of a "give-away" ceremony is appreciated. In his study of "potlatches" among the Kwakuitl of the Pacific Northwest, I. Goldman notes that "Gifts, such as animal skins, become symbolic of the interconnection between all spheres of life. . . . Exchange brings into connection the contemporary and natural world and the mythic world of the ancestors." This statement demonstrates that, much like the Den'a, the world of other Native People also have seen and unseen realms where all things are connected.

This connection supports the life cycle of the Den'a, who have in place an indigenous method to maintain the social order. By accepting one another for who they are and accepting ourselves for where we are, the Den'a exhibit a healing force that returns you to normal growth, development, and function.

For further reading, see: Coyhis 1993; Cruikshank 1990; Dall 1870; Goldman 1975; Haviland 1990; Lyons 1964; Mauss 1990; Nelson 1899; Schneider 1989; Shavanda 1987; Simeone 1990; Sullivan 1936; and VanStone 1974.

Tlingit

Nora Marks Dauenhauer and
Richard Dauenhauer

7.

Tlingit Lawrence Shields of the Cape Fox tribe beats a drum as totem pole carver Lee Wallace's Brown Bear pole is raised at Westmark/ Cape Fox lodge on April 5, 1991, in Ketchikan. Photo Hall Anderson, 1991.

The Tlingit Indians live in southeast Alaska from Yakutat to Dixon Entrance, predominantly on the coast, but also with inland communities in southwest Yukon and northwest British Columbia. A variety of evidence as well as Tlingit tradition suggest that the Tlingits migrated to the coast at an early date and spread from the southern range of their territory to the north, where they were expanding toward the Copper River at the time of European contact.

The relationship of Tlingit to other Native American languages is uncertain. There is great cultural similarity between Tlingit and adjacent Northwest Coast groups but no obvious linguistic affinity. On the other hand, many features of Tlingit phonology and grammar systematically parallel Athapaskan languages (including Navajo), but there are few similarities in vocabulary. Most linguists believe that Tlingit is genetically related to the Athapaskan family of

languages and that the recently extinct Eyak language and nearly extinct Tongass dialect of Tlingit are the "missing links" in the Na-Dene language chain. Still, the origin of much of the Tlingit vocabulary remains a puzzle.

Coastal Tlingits live in and on the edge of a rain forest, and this environment has shaped their distinctive lifestyle, material culture, and intellectual culture. Tlingit people use the food resources of the land and sea, especially salmon, seal, deer, and berries. Trees are important in art. Native American culture of the Northwest Coast has captured the imagination of explorers ever since first contact. These are the people of totem poles, elaborately carved wooden bowls and bentwood boxes, plank houses, ocean-going canoes, Chilkat robes, button blankets, and other well-known cultural objects

and events, especially the ceremony known in Tlingit as *koo.éex'*, and in English as "potlatch." Many features of these cultures, especially totem poles and potlatch, have often been misunderstood. The unifying factor in Tlingit folklife is the social structure, which determines the function of verbal and visual art, and the patterns of social and ritual interaction.

Social Structure: Moiety, Clan, and House Group

All of Tlingit society is organized into two reciprocating divisions, called moieties, named Raven and Eagle. Raven is sometimes known as Crow, and Eagle as Wolf. Crow and Wolf may be older terms. In contrast to clans, moieties have no political organization or power, but exist for the purposes of exogamy (regulation of marriage) and exchange of ritual services. Traditionally, a person married into the opposite moiety, although this pattern is no longer strictly observed. The moieties also group the clans for other kinds of reciprocal actions. For example, Ravens not only marry Eagles, but address songs and speeches to them as well. Eagles commission Raven artists to create visual art. Raven and Eagle clans host each other at potlatches, and engage in reciprocal ritual display of visual and verbal art representing the spirit world. Each moiety consists of many clans. Most clans are dispersed though a number of communities, but in any given community certain clans predominate for historical reasons. Political organization rests at the clan level; clans own heraldic crests, personal names, and other property.

Clans are further subdivided into house groups, sometimes called "lineage" in anthropological literature. Simply stated, the house where people lived or once lived was part of their identity. Historically the term referred to both residence and kinship, but now it is only a term of kinship, for not all members of a house group physically reside in the ancestral house, not all residents of a clan house are members of that house group, and few of the original houses are still standing.

Tlingit society is matrilineal, which means it is organized through the mother's line. A Tlingit is born into his or her mother's moiety, clan, and house group. The father's clan is just as significant, but it functions in a different way. While a person belongs to his or her mother's clan, he or she is also known as a "child of" the father's clan. This concept is basic to any serious understanding of Tlingit culture. Most songs, especially love songs, are addressed to members of the opposite moiety, who are identified according to their fathers' clan rather than their mothers' and their own.

Ownership and Reciprocity

Two main features characterize Tlingit culture and folk arts: ownership and reciprocity (or balance). Songs, stories, artistic designs, personal names, land, and other elements of Tlingit life are considered the property of a particular clan. The Tlingit term for this concept of tangible and intangible property is *at.óow.*

The patterns of visual art and oral literature follow and reinforce the patterns of social structure. The two moieties, Eagle and Raven, balance each other. In host-guest relationships at ceremonials, they share in each other's joy and work to remove each other's grief, matching song with song, speech with speech, and display of art piece with display of art piece. The exchange of speeches between the two moieties follows the pattern of exchange of marriage, goods,

and services, and the images in the songs and speeches are built around references of relationship to the opposite moiety. A song or speech by a host must be answered by a guest so that the words may be received formally. Within the speeches themselves, information and images may be balanced artistically and emotionally: physical and spiritual, living and departed, humans and animals, living creatures and the land.

The Concept of *At.óow*

At.óow is probably the single most important spiritual and cultural concept in Tlingit folklife. The word literally means "an owned or purchased object." This may be land (geographic features such as a mountain, a landmark, an historical site, a place such as Glacier Bay), a heavenly body (the sun, the Big Dipper, the Milky Way), a spirit, a personal name, an artistic design, or a range of other objects or things. It can be an image from oral literature, such as an episode from the Raven cycle on a tunic, hat, robe, or blanket; it can be a story or song about an event in the life of an ancestor. Ancestors can themselves be *at.óow.* *At.óow* can also be spirits of various kinds: shaman spirits and spirits of animals, trees, and geographic features. Through purchase by an ancestor, an "object" is owned by his or her descendants.

When asked why Tlingit people feel so strongly about *at.óow,* Tlingit bead artist Emma Marks replied, "*At.óow* is our life." The Tlingit word she used was *haa kusteeyí,* which translates as "our culture," "our way of life," or "life itself." For the Tlingit people, art and other *at.óow* are inseparable from life itself. Its sources are in nature, and its functions are spiritual and social. We cannot conduct our traditional ceremonies or make speeches in a spiritual context without them.

Ceremonial Display

The traditional art pieces called *at.óow* are brought out only on special occasions, usually in a ceremonial context, the most widely known of which, called "potlatch" in English, is a memorial ceremony involving ritual distribution of food and gifts. In Tlingit tradition, the ceremonial is called *koo.éex'* ("invitation"). It begins with a ritual called *L S'aatí Sháa Gaaxí* ("the widow's cry"), during which guests bring out the *at.óow* of their clan to wipe away the tears of the hosts. This ritual display of visual art is accompanied by oratory delivered by selected individuals who are genealogically related to the deceased, and by songs. When we put the *at.óow* on our grandchildren, we wrap them in our care; when we wear them, we know that our ancestors are present. When we do this, we are doing what the art was designed and created to do. We are also imitating our ancestors, doing things in remembrance of them.

This is the greatest honor we can give to them, and to our relatives among the hosting clan.

This ritual display shows how serious our art is, how it goes beyond mere form, and how strongly we feel about our *at.óow.* Each piece records and alludes to an historical and spiritual event; each piece of visual art is associated with songs that can be heard, dances that can be seen, and spirits that are neither seen nor heard except as manifested in the performance. All visual art, but especially the older pieces that are *at.óow,* is a very important ingredient to our lives and helps us to survive spiritually.

Art and Land

Our art, with its attendant system of *at.óow,* is also the spiritual and social element that holds our people and land together. Tlingit art is inseparable from the land. The designs are usually images of animals, places, or spirits associated with the places. Art materials come from the land and sea: wood, abalone, cedar bark, mountain goat wool, sheep horn, spruce roots, silver, copper, and gold. As we gather food and raw materials for art in our subsistence economy, we maintain close contact with our environment, and this intimate relationship is reflected in the form and content of our art. We know our animals by having close contact with them when we hunt them and when we prepare them for use. We learn early how to prepare each animal we skin. We know the skeletal forms. This is reflected in our art.

Our art comes from various levels of our experience: the first-hand knowledge of animals gained by participation in a subsistence economy; the knowledge of where we are and the history of where we have been; the sacred knowledge of legend and myth; the social knowledge of ourselves as family, house group, clan, and nation. In all these ways, as Tlingit elder and artist Emma Marks observed, "Our *at.óow* is our life."

For further reading, see: Dauenhauer and Dauenhauer 1987, 1990; de Laguna 1972; Emmons 1991; Kan 1989; and Olson 1991.

8, 9, 10.

"Dragon," "Tiger," and "Hawk" birch panels by Nanai artist Liudmila Ivanovna Passar from Komsomolsk-na-Amure, Siberia, 1991. Plywood and birch, Khabarovsk Regional Museum, Russia, #VX-310, VX-311, and VX-312. 31x34.5 cm each.

These three panels represent the totems of the Amur peoples. Mudur, the Dragon, master of the blue planet earth, is the ancestor of all living things.

Amba, the Tiger, son of a human woman named Khaposal and father of a human boy, Mokha, is the master of the taiga and the ancestor and protector of the Nanai. The most ancient clans of the Amur basin (Beldy, Akmanko, and Samar) are Tiger.

Gusi, the Hawk, became the ancestor of the Amur Evenk by flying down from the sky to a young woman, the only survivor of a horrible epidemic, and giving her three sons. The boys decided to move from the Gorin River and settled on the Amur River.

Native Peoples of the Russian Far East

Igor Krupnik

Thousands of years ago, the indigenous people who inhabited the Pacific gateways of Siberia made a historic breakthrough toward a more settled life on the coast. Those ancient Siberians, predominantly nomadic caribou hunters and fishermen, started to move to the seashore for a few months every spring or summer to hunt marine mammals, fish for migrating salmon, and collect bird eggs, seaweeds, and shellfish on the beaches.

In that new pattern, they followed general shift of Native people of the North Pacific region, who, one by one, turned to coastal life and to the abundant and far more stable resources of the sea. This maritime-focused economy spread along both the Siberian and American sides of the North Pacific, from Japan, Sakhalin Island, and Kamchatka to British Columbia and Washington State, like a giant arc connecting the two continents.

The northernmost section of this North Pacific cultural rim was occupied by the ancestors of present-day Yupik Eskimos and Aleuts in Western Alaska and of several Native nations in northeastern Siberia: Koryak, Itelmen, Chukchi, Nivkh, and Asiatic or Siberian Eskimos. They all shared a number of cultural developments and adaptations. Their economy became a flexible mixture of three major components: hunting for sea mammals, either from boats or on ice; hunting for land mammals (caribou, moose, elk, grizzly and polar bear, etc.) and birds; and fishing. They mastered dog-sled driving and built sophisticated boats of skin and wood propelled by paddles and sails. When they settled on the coast, they started to live in permanent, socially organized villages consisting of several dwellings—sod houses or dugouts in winter, skin or birch-bark tents and wooden plank houses in summer. In time, they developed elaborate rituals and community festivals and produced decorated fur and gutskin clothing, skin drums, wooden masks, and ivory carvings.

Not all indigenous Siberians moved to the coast. Some remained inland and preserved their original lifestyle of nomadic hunting and fishing. The people of the Siberian interior created a fairly distinct cultural universe, due to the continuous influx of migrants from regions farther inland. These "inlanders" contributed cultural patterns, beliefs, and subsistence practices that originated in the forests and tundra of northern Asia. Of those, by far the greatest development in aboriginal life in Siberia was the domestication of reindeer.

There are several theories on the origin of indigenous reindeer herding, but few clues tell us when it spread to the Pacific margins of Siberia. It probably happened shortly before Russians came to the area in the mid-1600s. Mastering reindeer herding was the second most important economic revolution for Siberian Native people, after mastering the resources of the sea.

The herders' life followed the annual cycle of the reindeer, with seasonal migrations for pasture grounds over hundreds of miles. People started to travel and to transport their belongings on domesticated reindeer, to live on reindeer meat and fat, to make clothing and tents of reindeer hide, and to get everything they needed by exchanging reindeer products with their neighbors.

Through the barter process, Native life in northeastern Siberia became highly specialized. Coastal people focused even more on marine hunting and fishing; the mainland folk—Even, Evenk, Yukaghir, and the inland groups of Chukchi and Koryak—became nomadic herdsmen or reindeer-driven hunters. As a result, interior folkways and art were influenced by a new mode of life, while ceremonies focused on domestic reindeer occupied the pivotal place in local worldviews and festivals. As time passed, those two basic traditions, the interior and the coastal, cross-bred at several locations along the Siberian Pacific area. That mixture produced a thriving diversity of lifestyles and artistic expression, which has survived into the present as the priceless cultural legacy of Native Siberians.

Siberian Yupik

Igor Krupnik

Siberian Yupik performing an eider duck ceremony. Model ducks slide on lines controlled by the participants while they blow mouth whistles that sound like shrill cries of eiders. Photo W. Bogoras, Spring 1901. Jesup Expedition. American Museum of Natural History neg. #1322.

The closest kin to Native Alaskans live just across the Bering Strait, along the coast of Siberia's Chukchi Peninsula. They are known as Asiatic Eskimo in Russia and as Siberian Yupik in America. As direct cultural heirs of the ancient coastal dwellers at the crossroads of continents, they form the west-ernmost population within the Eskimo/Inuit cultural area, which extends from Bering Strait to Greenland. Asiatic Eskimos present-ly number about 1,700; they are closely related to the Yupik-speaking inhabitants of St. Lawrence Island and nearby western Alaska.

Asiatic Eskimos call themselves Yupigyt ("the real people"). During the 1600s and 1700s, they lived all along the Siberian side of the Bering Strait, on the Arctic coast of the Chukchi Peninsula, and south on the Bering Sea shores. Their neighbors, the interior Chukchi people, gradually pushed them out of this area, until they finally retreated to the mountainous promontories at the sout eastern and northeastern edges of the Chukchi Peninsula. The southern branch of Siberian Yupik, around the modern town of Provideniia, is linguistically and culturally akin to the people of St. Lawrence Island. The northern group, who formerly lived at the rocky East Cape (Cape Dezhnev), maintained close contacts with the American Natives of the Bering Strait narrows—the Diomede and King islanders and people of Wales, Alaska.

Siberian Yupik, like the residents of St. Lawrence, Diomede, and King islands, used to live in large permanent coastal villages and rarely engaged in inland activities. They were first and foremost sea-mammal hunters, skilled in harvesting walruses, seals, and large whales, using multi-seat skin boats equipped with paddles and gut sails. During the 1800s they changed their traditional dwellings from sod houses and communal dugouts to large tents made of walrus hide and known by the Chukchi word *iaranga*. Their diet was based on walrus, seal, and whale meat and blubber, supplemented by fish, birds, beach products, and reindeer meat bartered from reindeer-men of the interior. This style of life was virtually the same as that of ancient Bering Strait hunters of past millennia (except for bartering for reindeer meat, which was previously supplied by caribou hunting).

Despite active contacts with American whalers and traders in the late 1800s, Siberian Yupik retained their lifestyle well into the present century. Their communities were organized along the lines of patrilineal clans that dominated social networks and ceremonial activities. Elaborate rituals, including whale and walrus festivals, with sacrifices and exchanges of gifts, were arranged as thanksgiving to sea and animal spirits. Communal dancing and shamanistic performances accompanied by group singing and drum-beating thrived on Siberian shores even in the 1930s, unopposed by Christian missionaries, in contrast to the situation among Native Alaskans on the other side of Bering Strait.

Wood is scarce on Siberia's rocky Arctic coasts, but walrus ivory, fur, and hides are abundant as raw material for art, and a

tradition sprang up of gorgeous ivory carving and ornamented fur clothing. European contacts spurred souvenir production—decorated tusks, ivory figurines, models of skin boats, fur carpets and slippers. People stayed strong and proud in their ethnic roots, in the close relations they maintained with the spirits of their land and sea, and of the animals they hunted.

Since the 1930s, this vibrant culture has undergone dramatic changes under the pressure of acculturation. The Soviet regime closed small villages and camps, and moved residents to larger villages of prefabricated wooden houses, with modern schools, clinics, and community buildings. Small Native cooperatives, started in the 1920s, were gradually absorbed into large state-run farms devoted to commercial fox-farming and supplying the inland reindeer industry. Sea-mammal hunting and fishing were reduced to secondary activities. Native whaling became extinct by the 1950s or 1960s, and traditional rituals and hunting ceremonies eroded altogether.

Yupik villages became dominated by outsiders. Shamans were oppressed as "class enemies," while Yupik children and youngsters accepted the new ideology of communist society. Since the 1960s, children no longer speak the Native language, and the authority of elders, once revered for their knowledge of ritual and survival, was supplanted by Russian bureaucrats and Communist functionaries. As a result, Siberian Yupik society disintegrated under government policies of planned economy and paternalistic protection. The young, the middle-aged, and the elderly were equally cut adrift from participation in their own fates.

A few components of Native life survived, nevertheless, including some hunting for seals and walruses from skin and wood boats, food-sharing, subsistence plant-gathering, and dog-sled driving. The Native diet is still based mainly on fish and sea-mammal meat, and winter clothing—at least for hunters and elders—is still made of traditional reindeer and seal skins. Some Yupik cultural hall-marks, such as group dancing, decorative ivory carving, and souvenir skin production, even received governmental financial support under a Soviet policy aimed at protecting Arctic Natives.

The revival of Siberian Yupik culture was spurred in the late 1980s when the "Ice Curtain" dividing Bering Strait was broken. Contacts quickly resumed between Siberian Yupik and Native Alaskans, particularly between Yupik communities from Provideniia Bay and St. Lawrence Island. Since then, communications have boomed, propelled by regular group and family visits, air and boat crossings, and even direct telephone lines. The Siberian Eskimo's official return to the international Arctic Native community was achieved in 1989, when a Soviet Eskimo delegation attended the Inuit Circumpolar Conference meeting in Greenland, to become a part of the ICC political and cultural network.

For this Siberian Yupik revival, Russia's current economic crisis bodes a future of uncertainty and distress. As the centralized state economy disintegrates, so does the entire former system of employment, technology and food supplies, and cash flow. Dependence on state subsidies, a shortage of grassroots political skills, and a lack of autonomy in economic and civic decisions prevent Yupik communities from implementing any alternative strategies for their future.

The struggle for more control through self-government has become a key issue. Siberian Yupik people must renegotiate their place in a local administrative system formerly dominated by Russians and other outsiders, and they must build a new balance of power at community and district levels. As current economic problems drive outsiders from the area, local people are steadily regaining their numerical advantage, prestige, and political muscle. Under such a trend, Siberian Yupik communities may implement new models of economic and social organization, perhaps with the help of their relatives and partners across Bering Strait.

For further reading, see: Achirgina-Arsiak 1992; Hughes 1984; Krupnik 1987 and 1988; and Voblov 1959.

Chukchi

Igor Krupnik

The Chukchi are the largest Native nation (about 15,000) on the Asian side of the North Pacific. At present, they populate a huge area that reaches from Bering Strait to the Kolyma River valley deep in inland Siberia, and extends along both the Arctic and Pacific coasts of northeast Asia. Their name was given to them by Russians, who also bestowed it on the Chukchi Peninsula, Chukchi Sea, Chukchi Autonomous Area, and the Chukchi District, which faces Alaska across Bering Strait.

The Russian name "Chukchi" actually comes from the Chukchi word *Chauchu* ("rich in reindeer"). Reindeermen use this word to distinguish themselves from coastal folk, who are usually called *Anqallyt* ("the sea people"). During the Soviet era, a new Chukchi name was introduced for the entire nation—*Luoravetlans* ("the real people").

Although an indigenous Siberian nation, the Chukchi apparently came to Bering Strait later than the Eskimos. anthropologists trace their origin to the ancient residents of interior and coastal Siberia, around the northern Okhotsk Sea, that is, about a thousand miles from Bering Strait. Their closest kin are the Koryak people of northern Kamchatka, with whom the Chukchi share similarities in language, beliefs, and historical tradition.

Originally caribou hunters and inland fishermen, many Chukchi have successfully adapted to an Eskimo-like lifestyle and culture. Those people of inland stock who settled on the coast and took up walrus and whale hunting are known as Maritime Chukchi. Many are genetically descended from Eskimos who mixed with the Chukchi and were assimilated by them. The old Eskimo legacy, however, became part of Coastal Chukchi culture, as seen in its ceremonies, dances, folktales, and beliefs.

Those Chukchi who retained their original inland lifestyle became reindeer herders. In the 1700s, these were the warlike nomads who stopped Russian colonial expansion at the gateways of America by fierce and successful military resistance. Raiding bands of Chukchi warriors confronted Russian parties, refused to pay the fur-tribute to the authorities, and destroyed Native groups who were loyal to the Russians. In order to subjugate the Chukchi by force, Russia sent several military expeditions in the early 1700s, but all were defeated, and Russia withdrew from the area for more than a century. Russian Orthodox missionaries were no more successful in converting Chukchi to Christianity and challenging their indigenous traditions. In the 1800s, the Reindeer Chukchi were twice as numerous as the Asiatic Eskimos and Maritime Chukchi combined.

As the most powerful local nation, Chukchi are strong in their ethnic identity and proud of their cultural roots. In their former relations with neighboring Native tribes, they normally obliged others to learn their language. Their high status was built on military power and wealth in reindeer herds, which made other Natives depend upon them for food, furs, and clothing. The image of "authentic reindeer folk," never subjugated by anybody, is still a dominant part of the Chukchi mentality.

The Chukchi traditional worldview, like that of the Siberian Yupik, was dominated by the idea that all nature is animated, and all things—animals, birds, trees, and even stones—have spirit "masters." The world is inhabited by numerous spirits and malicious creatures who can influence human well-being and the normal courses of life. Success in hunting, reindeer herding, traveling, and other activities mostly depends upon the goodwill of "animal masters" and local land spirits. By rituals and observances, people can generally get along with the supernatural world. Real communication, however, is maintained by the rare few, the shamans, assisted by their personal "helping spirits." Images of spirits and mythological creatures are very common in Chukchi drawings and decorative art.

According to traditional Chukchi cosmology, several "worlds"—from five to seven, or nine—are situated one above another. While the earth is inhabited by living humans and animals, the upper and lower worlds are populated by malicious spirits, deceased people, or special types of "upper" and "lower" beings. Ordinary people must spend their lives in the present reality, but shamans could move freely between the earth and the upper and lower worlds during seances. Many Chukchi folktales and art objects represent a shaman's journey through the various physical and spiritual worlds.

The Reindeer Chukchi of the interior were among the last Siberian Natives to give up their language, beliefs, and rituals under the pressure of acculturation. In some remote areas, shamanistic performances and ceremonies continued well into the Communist era. But since the 1950s, Soviet officials have compelled thousands of former herdsmen to settle along the coast in large modernized villages. Here, their former preference for the free nomadic life quickly eroded, and they mixed with Maritime Chukchi, Eskimos, and Russian newcomers.

Due to their numerical strength and a greater share in local and Soviet power structures, the Coastal Chukchi have good prospects for building some form of self-government at village and even district levels. With the demise of a Russian-controlled administration, new Chukchi leaders will soon emerge as an alternative regional political force. On the other hand, the Chukchi lack the Siberian Yupik's network of personal and cultural ties with Native Alaskans and a shared language that greatly facilitates international contacts.

The Reindeer Chukchi of the interior must address a different set of political targets. Their reindeer economy is viable, and there is no power to share in the tundra wilderness, since few Russians live in the interior beyond a handful of mining and rural communities. The main battle so far is focused upon privatizing reindeer herds presently monopolized by state farms. As the new property system for reindeer becomes established, whether as cooperative, family, or even private herding enterprises, the issue of land claims, pasture allocation, and compensation for lost and polluted grazing areas will eventually surface as the main political priority.

The biggest threat to the revival of Reindeer Chukchi is the generation gap induced by decades of Soviet acculturation. Although older people rooted in Native tradition are numerous and respected, the middle-aged and younger generations are now attached to a more comfortable village life. Raised in Soviet boarding schools, they lack the experience and stamina of real tundra herdsmen. The survival of Chukchi culture and language depends upon the success of hundreds of current village residents in returning to their former lifestyle.

For further reading, see: Antropova and Kuznetsova 1964; Arutiunov 1988a; and Bogoras 1909.

Koryak

Igor Krupnik

13.

Koryak family at the village of Verkhnii-Paren'. Photo Sergei Khalanskii, about 1990.

ultural affinities between Native Siberians and Native Alaskans go far beyond the Bering Strait area. Anthropologists have found striking parallels between the myths, rituals, and dwelling types of the Koryak—inhabitants of the Kamchatka Peninsula—and those of Tlingit, Tsimshian, and other Native peoples of America's Northwest Coast.

The central figure of Koryak mythology is Big-Raven (Quikil or Quikinnaqu), who appears as the first man, the father and protector of the Koryak, as well as a powerful shaman and a supernatural being. As the Great Transformer of the world, Big-Raven presides at every shamanistic ceremony. Almost all Koryak myths and folktales deal with the life, travels, adventures, and tricks of Big-Raven and his family. About 80 percent of those episodes have parallels in the mythology of the Northwest Coast indigenous peoples.

These similarities have led researchers to seek ancient cultural connections or even a common origin for these peoples separated by the North Pacific. Koryak (as well as neighboring Itelmen and Chukchi) were once called "Americanoids" and were thought to be return migrants from America to Siberia, after the initial peopling of the New World. Although this hypothesis lacks proof beyond similarities in myths and beliefs, Koryak-Northwest Coast affinities are still a key subject for research.

The Kamchatka Peninsula is a huge extension of land that stretches for 1,000 miles into the Pacific, separating the Bering and Okhotsk seas. The land is mountainous and volcanic, covered by tundra shrubs in the north and by coniferous forest in the south. It possesses the most abundant resources in all Siberia for feeding people— deer, moose, Dall sheep, fur-bearing and marine mammals, shellfish, and above all, bounteous runs of Pacific salmon.

The indigenous people of this land are the Koryak, who live at and around the northern stem of the peninsula, and the Itelmen, former inhabitants of its central and southern section. Like the Chukchi, the Koryak are divided between coastal maritime hunters and inland nomadic herders. Before the arrival of Russians, Itelmen were predominantly river fishermen. Once numerous and militant, the Itelmen were nearly destroyed by contact. Their population dwindled to the present count of 2,500 people, and their legacy all but perished under the pressure of epidemics and acculturation. Despite heavy losses, the Koryak managed to preserve their traditions.

The Koryak occupy a special position within the Siberian portion of the Pacific Rim. They used to live at the very intersection of all cultural influences entering the Siberian Pacific from various directions. Along the coast, Koryak land lay between the Eskimo and Aleut sea-mammal hunting area to the north, and the Itelmen, Nivkh, and Ainu Pacific salmon-fishing area to the south. The inland portion of the Koryak tribe lies between the arctic tundra, where Reindeer Chukchi follow their herds, and the Even/Tungus area of subsistence hunting and fishing in the northern forests. This unique combination of neighbors has brought various legacies into Koryak culture.

Originally, the Koryak did not call themselves by that name, and the origin the word is unknown. The Russians may have introduced it in the late 1600s when they first met with the Reindeer portion of the tribe, since the word means "(being) with reindeer."

The Koryak had no common tribal name. The coastal people were called Nemelan ("village dwellers"), while the reindeer herders preferred the name Chauchen or Chauchuven ("rich in reindeer," the same as the Chukchi word Chauchu).

By the time of their first contacts with Russians in the 1650s, the Koryak, unlike Chukchi, did not have an integrated nation with a common language and identity. The interior herders were actually a separate folk of several nomadic bands, with a dialect of their own. Coastal dwellers were divided into a dozen regional groups, each having a dialect distinct from that of the reindeer people. This deep split helped Russians to incorporate Kamchatka residents, despite their strenuous resistance, into a Siberian administrative system by the early 1700s.

Taxation, christianization, and epidemics soon followed. Half of the Koryak (and all Itelmen) converted to the Russian Orthodox Church. While the reindeer people mostly preserved their original lifestyle, the coastal groups became more assimilated. Small farms and livestock were introduced among southern Koryak and Itelmen. People moved from underground dwellings to log houses and gave up indigenous fur clothing for Russian-style garments. Although salmon still dominated the Native diet, bread, flour, and potatoes became popular. Local edible plants and berries, formerly of great importance, were gradually replaced by introduced vegetables.

As Soviet power became established on Siberia's Pacific coast, the entire Koryak territory was declared a Koryak Autonomous Area in 1931. Following the new governmental policy, modern administrative posts were built, schools were introduced, and Native villages were reorganized as collective farms for commercial fishing, trapping, and herding.

To forge a new nation out of a dozen tribal divisions, Soviet administrators supported the idea of a "general" Koryak ethnicity. They introduced a written Koryak language based on a Reindeer Koryak dialect, which was incomprehensible to coastal Koryak. Russians and other newcomers streamed into the area and transformed Koryak villages into mixed communities. In 1956 Native education was abandoned altogether.

The influx of outsiders turned the Koryak nation (presently 9,000 people) into a minority on their own land. Smaller villages were closed, and their residents were relocated to larger new communities with mixed populations. Continuing resettlement uprooted most of the former Koryak tribal divisions, and the entire nation was placed under enormous pressure to assimilate.

But that very policy finally triggered a revival. When a tiny community of Paren' Koryak refused to abandon their old village in 1985, the story of Paren' resistance attracted attention from the media, from other Koryak, and even from international Native organizations. In the late 1980s, Koryak activists gained political momentum. A Koryak Native association has been created, and in 1990 the Koryak Autonomous Area seceded from Kamchatka Province to become an independent member of the Russian Federation.

The Koryak's political agenda is similar to that of the Chukchi, being split into separate "coastal" and "interior" streams. Unlike the Chukchi, however, the Koryak still lack a common ethnic identity and language. Therefore, issues of regional interest as opposed to general Koryak loyalty will be extremely acute. To make things worse, the Koryak area has few commercial resources beyond fishing, and a collapse in local industries, services, and transportation could be a real challenge to a small nation. Since Russians are now fleeing the area, Koryak land may soon return to its original owners—but in a state of recession and economic despair.

For further reading, see: Antropova 1964; Arutiunov 1988b; Jochelson 1908; and Krasheninnikov 1972.

Even

Igor Krupnik

14.

Even celebration in April, Bilibino district, Chukotka. Photo Sergei Khalanskii, about 1990.

The interior part of the Siberian Pacific, rarely visited by coastal dwellers, is dominated by people of a different stock. The Russians called them Tungus. This general name covers a great number of Native tribes that populated central and eastern Siberia from the Pacific shore, through five time zones, deep into inner Asia. Their languages belong to the same linguistic stock as the Manchu people of northern China; this makes the

Tungus distant relatives of nomadic Turkic and Mongolic nations, the herdsmen and fierce warriors of the Eurasian steppe.

The ancient Tungus originated somewhere on the northeastern fringe of the steppe, probably between Lake Baikal and the upper Amur River. From this region, they moved north into the Siberian forest (or taiga) to become its complete masters and most skilled users. In their northward trek, the Tungus tribes assimilated some ancient

The people who were most completely swept up by this gradual Tungus invasion were the Yukaghir, a few of whom survive as a small hunting nation in the remote areas of northeastern Siberia.

Despite mixing with local tribes, Tungus culture remained mostly intact. Its four major components are: reindeer herding, using reindeer as riding and pack animals; extensive hunting of land game; a style of hide clothing that includes a leather apron and a fur parka cut like a 19th-century European morning coat; and social organization based on patrilineal clans with strict marriage regulations.

In their age-old move through the mountains and forests of inner Siberia, the Tungus tribes gradually split into three major clusters. Those who moved northward and westward formed the largest portion, today known as Evenk (current population 30,000 in Russia and about 20,000 in northern China). Those who moved eastward—to eastern Yakutia, Kolyma River, and the northern Okhotsk Sea—called themselves Even (presently about 17,000). Migrants into the Amur River basin mixed with local tribes and formed a number of small fishing and hunting nations, which are described in the chapter on Amur River peoples.

This original distribution of the Tungus tribes was modified by a number of later migrations. Some groups of Evenk, fleeing Russian invaders, moved to the Amur River valley, the southern coast of the Okhotsk Sea, and Sakhalin Island.

The Even, like all Tungus peoples, are fairly recent arrivals in the North Pacific region. In some areas they first arrived just before or soon after the Russian invasion in the mid-1600s. Experienced warriors and reindeer riders armed with iron lances and Russian firearms, they pushed back their less powerful neighbors, especially local Yukaghir and Koryak. The Even drive continued throughout Russian colonial rule, until they covered the Kolyma River valley, the Anadyr River basin, and the interior of the Kamchatka Peninsula.

The Even's traditional economy, as part of the original Tungus pattern, focused on reindeer herding and land game hunting. In both activities, reindeer were important as riding and pack animals. Even reindeer are large, strong, and fully tamed, unlike those raised by Chukchi and Koryak herders. Well trained to bear a good-sized rider, an Even reindeer can carry a load of 80 kilograms (180 pounds) and travel 50 miles a day. The Even herds, however, were of relatively small size, numbering in the dozens or a few hundreds. To ride reindeer, Even used a special saddle and a harness similar to

that used by the horse-riding peoples of inner Asia. They never milk reindeer and rarely use sledges for driving, unlike Chukchi, Koryak, and other Siberian herdsmen. The Even are renowned through the Siberian Pacific as experienced land and fur-game hunters. After the arrival of Russians, they became actively engaged in fur-trapping and trade for sable, marten, fox, and squirrel pelts. Subsistence hunting concentrated on large meat animals, such as elk, wild reindeer of the forest and tundra, deer, bear, and mountain sheep. Fishing and fowl hunting was far less important, except in coastal areas with good salmon runs.

The Even made clothing of reindeer and elk skin, fancily decorated with beads, reindeer and elk hair embroidery, and small metal ornaments. All items—leather apron, gloves, hide leggings, caps, borders of hide coats—were elegantly ornamented. Men's trousers are brief, rather Chinese in style, and need extra leg protectors for warmth—evidence that the Evens originally came from the south.

Another piece of evidence for the "inner Siberian" origin of the Even is their traditional social system. Unlike most Native peoples of the Pacific coasrland, Even were organized into a network of patrilineal clans, and strict rules forbade marriages within a clan. Clan members might be scattered over a huge territory, but they steadfastly preserved their clan affiliation and patrilineal descent. Normally, two or more clans formed a marriage unit in which cross-cousin marriage was the preferred pattern. In former times, Even always migrated in bands that included members of various clans to ensure intermarriage. Many Even clans were actually of Yukaghir origin, while several Even were also incorporated into Yukaghir clans.

In the 1700s Even converted to the Russian Orthodox Church and soon became devout Christians. Children were regularly baptized, and marriages were licensed by Orthodox priests. Russian-style family and personal names replaced original Even names, and members of a patrilineal clan all took the same last name. Through conversion, Even beliefs mixed with Christian values and legends, though some shamanistic practices survived, and shamans were respected as spiritual leaders. "Shaman" is actually a Tungus word; the Russians introduced it to other European languages.

By the early 1800s Even were fully dependent on trade with Russians for various goods, including ammunition, tea, tobacco, flour, and bread. Russian pressure on the Even increased dramatically in the 1930s, when the new Soviet state launched numerous industrial projects in northeastern Siberia using a labor force of thousands of convicts. An Even "autonomous area" was declared in 1931 but soon abolished. The entire valley of the Kolyma River was gradually transformed into a zone of gold-mining, logging, and prison camps. Even hunting bands retreated into remote areas, but eventually they were brought under Soviet administration and merged into a state-run economy of herding and trapping.

The Even nation is now in a desperate situation. The newly formed Association of the Native People of Chukotka and Kolyma (ANPCK) recognizes Even culture as severely "damaged." State-run mines and industrial zones cover traditional hunting and grazing areas. Although strong in numbers, the Even population is scattered (about 17,000 in Yakutia, Magadan, and Kamchatka provinces). There are few communities where Even are numerous enough to start education and cultural activities in their Native language. Even political power in the Pacific provinces of Siberia is very limited and centered around a newly-established Even section within the ANPCK. Because of this, the Even political agenda is focused on preserving Native lands and on lobbying for government support in language, education, and other related programs for cultural survival.

For further reading, see: Arutiunov 1988c; Jochelson 1926; Kreynovich 1979; Levin and Vasil'yev 1964; and Service 1978.

Amur River Peoples

Igor Krupnik

The southernmost portion of the Siberian Pacific, once part of the ancient empires of China and Korea, is formed by the lower Amur basin. The Amur River is the largest in Siberia (about 2,700 miles), equal in size and might to Alaska's Yukon River. For ages, the Amur River served as a cultural "highway" along which peoples moved, exchanging and mixing customs, beliefs, and artistic traditions. The Amur was the main route of communication connecting the forests of the Siberian interior, the Pacific coastland, and even the remote shores of the Arctic Ocean. Migrations of peoples from China and the Central Asian steppe brought agriculture, animal husbandry, metalware, and pottery to the gateways of Siberia.

As an age-old cultural crossroad, the Amur basin has a complicated history. In distant prehistory, people settled in the river valley with its plentiful salmon runs. They lived by fishing, hunting, and plant gathering; later, around the first century B.C., the Manchu people of northern China introduced farming and animal breeding into the region.

Once agriculture was established in the fertile middle section of the Amur Basin, the population grew, and the area became the heartland of powerful empires. The Manchu people of the Middle Amur had fortified cities, an army, and a codified system of administration. The lower reaches of the river, however, where the climate was more severe, retained their original hunting and fishing economies. In the mid-1800s the river became an international border, separating the Russian empire on its northern bank from China to the south.

The Native people who inhabited the lower Amur valley were a mixture of various Tungus and Manchu tribes from the interior, Nivkh, and probably Ainu migrants from Sakhalin Island and the Amur estuary. Except for the Nivkh, all Native peoples of the Amur valley speak closely related languages of Tungus-Manchu stock. They share the same general name for themselves, *nani* ("local people"), and a number of clan names and clan groups cross ethnic lines. Presently, those nations are known as: Nanai (population 12,000), Ulchi (3,200), Udegei (1,900), Oroch (900), and Negidal (600). Another 1,500 Nanai and 4,000 Oroch live on the Chinese side of the Amur and along adjacent streams.

All Native peoples of the Amur valley practiced salmon fishing and hunting for land animals of the forest and for marine mammals on the coast and the Amur estuary. Groups that controlled good fishing grounds along the river—such as the Nanai and Ulchi—led more or less sedentary lives. Others—such as the Negidal, Udegei, and Oroch—tended to be hunters and followed a more mobile lifestyle. As river and estuary fishermen, Amur people were skilled in building various kinds of birchbark canoes and large wooden boats, up to 10 meters (25 feet) long. They were also experienced dog breeders and outstanding skiers, using skis lined with seal and reindeer skin in the deep snow of the northern forests.

Amur valley people were famous for elaborate clothing and footwear made of salmon fishskin. All clothing was gorgeously decorated, especially shamans' robes and festival garments. The decorations, often in many colors, show Chinese-style motifs, modified according to the local tradition for intricate designs.

Woodworking was another major local craft, using metal tools imported by Chinese, Korean, or Russian traders. Finely carved wooden dishes and boxes were made for both personal use and for sale, and various parts of dwellings, gravehouses, boats, and sledges were fancily decorated. Images of trees, dragons, tigers, and birds dominate in Native art. Birds—mainly waterfowl—were prominent in local myths about the creation of the universe and the construction of the "world trees" that link the upper, middle, and lower worlds.

Snakes also appear often in Amur art and folklore. According to Nanai legend, the earth was originally smooth and covered with water, until a giant serpent plowed deep valleys with his body. The water flowed down the valleys, leaving dry land for humans and other creatures. Snake images appear in Native art in the form of spirals and zigzags.

The Russians first entered the Amur valley in the mid-1600s, but Chinese troops drove them back for about 200 years. In the 1800s, Russia formally annexed the north side of the valley and all the lower portion. Russian peasants, settlers, and Orthodox missionaries soon poured into the area. Railroads, towns, and villages were built, while Native peoples were steadily forced to gather at a few locations within their tribal lands and to surrender their hunting and fishing grounds. Within fifty years, Native people were a minority among a booming population of Russian, Chinese, and Korean newcomers.

After Soviet power was established in the area, it tried to protect Native people by designating their traditional lands as territorial "autonomies." A handful of "Native districts" were created in the 1920s to boost Native political activity and participation in administration. Those districts were integrated into a larger Lower Amur "national area," following the pattern applied to other minority nations in Siberia.

But the valley, with its abundant fish and timber resources, was too important for Russian industry. The Lower Amur "national area" was soon annulled. "Native districts" lost their specific rights and gradually became ordinary precincts. Native languages

dwindled, as Native speakers had no say in public life. Although Native people received government funds to develop village schools, medical facilities, and economies, they were ever more outnumbered and overpowered throughout the area. The state supported Native salmon fisheries and fur trapping for economic reasons and promoted dancing and decorative arts to keep Native identity afloat.

That precarious balance was recently threatened by new plans for industry and development. Due to Russia's current economic crisis, local authorities are desperate for foreign investment. The hunger for funds is opening the door to any proposal backed by foreign cash. China is pushing for new construction and dam projects, to supply its growing population in the north. The outcome for the valley would be degradation of the environment, collapse of the salmon runs, and new pressure on Native peoples.

To protect their lifestyle, Amur River nations are becoming more assertive. In 1992 the Udegei gained worldwide attention through their staunch refusal to surrender tribal lands in the Bikin River valley to a Russian-Korean logging venture. Udegei village councils rejected the proposal and sent hunters to guard the borders of their land. The Udegei hired a lawyer to defend their rights and held public rallies outside government buildings. Several international groups, Russian activists, and government officials also rallied to support the Udegei. As of 1993, the Bikin valley logging project was delayed for further social and environmental evaluation.

For further reading, see: Black 1988; Ivanov, Levin, and Smolyak 1964a; Laufer 1902; and Okladnikov 1981.

Nivkh

Igor Krupnik

16.

Nivkh teacher Nukhba and students, reading newly published primer in the Nivkh language.

Only 10% of the Nivkh still know their native language, and most of these are over the age of fifty. Khabarovsk Arsenev Regional Museum.

As Siberia's Pacific coastland runs farther south, to the gateways of Japan and China, it splits in two, as if reflecting two different cultural streams. The eastern stretch turns into a narrow 700-mile-long strip—Sakhalin Island, whose southern tip nearly joins the island of Hokkaido, the northernmost portion of Japan. The western stretch follows the rocky coast of the present-day Russian Maritime Province and becomes the huge Amur River valley. The river streams into the

heart of the forests of inland Siberia, while its southern tributaries reach the borders of Korea and northern China. Sakhalin Island resembles a giant fish, with its head turned northward toward the mouth of the Amur River. Both mainland and island are inhabited by one Native Siberian nation—the Nivkh. Their present population of some 4,600 people is split almost evenly between the island and mainland.

The Nivkh, or Gilyak, as the older literature calls them, are a cultural mystery. Linguistically they are isolated, showing no direct affinities with their closest neighbors, the Ainu of Sakhalin Island and the Tungus and Manchu inhabitants of the Amur River region. Physically Nivkh also differ from the surrounding Siberian populations. In terms of subsistence, they are more like the Koryak and Itelmen, coastal sea-mammal hunters and fishermen of the Kamchatka Peninsula and northern Okhotsk Sea coast. On the other hand, certain features in ancient Nivkh spiritual culture reflect cultural connections with the people of the Northwest coast of North America.

According to Nivkh traditional beliefs, Sakhalin Island is actually a giant beast lying on its belly. Its back is covered by a thick "hair" of trees, and people live in that hair, like small insects. The beast's "head" is formed by the island's northernmost extension, Cape Mary, and its feet are two southern peninsulas stretching into the LaPerouse Strait. Periodically, the beast rises, as if bothered by the people on its back, like a sleeping dog. When the beast moves, people feel the earth trembling and roaring in earthquake.

The Nivkh shared Sakhalin Island with a few other Native nations. Their southern neighbors were Ainu who originally came from the island of Hokkaido, pushed northward by Japanese expansion. Ainu were inland hunters and fishermen with many cultural features that show their southern origin. Nivkh-Ainu relations were mainly hostile, as Nivkh raided Ainu villages for goods, women, and slaves.

The Nivkh's only northern neighbors were a tiny group of Tungus-speaking Orok (now about 600). They once came from the nearest mainland, with their small reindeer herds, and preserved the original Tungus subsistence pattern of hunting and fishing supplemented by small-scale reindeer breeding. In the 1800s another group of Tungus-speaking people migrated to the island—the reindeer-breeding Evenk (presently 200 people altogether), who also settled in the island's northern interior. Nivkh were also in contact with the Chinese, at least for the last few centuries, and since the 1700s with the Japanese as well. These contacts provided the Nivkh with metalware, tobacco, silk, manufactured clothing, beads, and porcelain in exchange for furs, fish-skin, and eagle feathers.

In contrast to their neighbors, the Nivkh displayed many cultural and subsistence adaptations that indicate a subarctic origin—or at least close contacts with arctic people. Their traditional winter dwelling was an earthen house built half-underground, entered by way of a smoke hole in the roof. Nivkh clothing was made of seal skins and animal furs. Hunting for seal, sea lion, and beluga whale from large wooden boats occupied a prominent role in Nivkh economy. Nivkh were renowned dog-breeders and dog-sled drivers. Dog sledding, a characteristic feature of arctic life, was adopted from the Nivkh by all their neighboring nations, the Ainu, Orok, and Amur River people. The Nivkh sled, their way of harnessing dogs, and their practice of driving a sled from a seated position are close to the Itelmen style and to Chukchi and Koryak reindeer driving.

Traditionally, Nivkh lived in clan-organized village communities that changed location two or three times a year. In the spring they traveled to the shore for sea-mammal hunting and salmon fishing; there they usually occupied wooden plank houses, often built on piles. In the fall they moved inland to winter settlements along the river valleys. More permanent dwellings were built at the winter site—semi-underground houses covered with earth and grass, or, later, large frame houses copied from the Manchu and Chinese.

The most distinctive feature of Nivkh ritual life was their famous "bear festival." Its climax was the sacrifice of a live bear, usually captured as a cub and raised in the village by a certain clan or lineage. Preparation for the festival lasted several years, while the captured bear grew to maturity in a specially built corral. The bear festival usually took place in winter and included—besides the ritual feeding and killing of the bear—dog races, group games, a communal feast, and group dances. The festival was given by a group of relatives to honor the death of a kinsman. Generally, it was an inter-clan ceremony in which a clan of wife-takers restored their connection with a clan of wife-givers—a connection broken by a kinsman's death. Several neighboring peoples—Ainu, Orok, Amur River nations—also practiced this tradition of bear sacrifice.

Nivkh contacts with the Russians began in the mid-1800s, when Sakhalin Island and the Amur River valley were incorporated into the Russian empire. Soon Russian peasants were sent to colonize Sakhalin, and in the 1880s the island was made a place of exile and convict labor. This continued into the first decades of the Soviet regime; several local industries, including logging, coal-mining, and oil, were manned primarily by convicts.

As Sakhalin's immigrant population grew, the government forced the Nivkh and other Native people out of their traditional lands through a series of resettlements. In 1946 all Sakhalin Ainu and half of all Orok were relocated to Japan. The Native residents of Sakhalin were overwhelmed by incoming Russians. At present, the Native people constitute barely 0.4 percent of the total island population of 700,000.

The breakdown of the Soviet state system and Russia's recent economic crisis placed a new threat to the Nivkh and other Native residents. Sakhalin Island is currently Russia's largest oil-producing area in the Pacific. There are several new plans to expand off-shore oil-drilling and to construct pipelines across the island to pump oil to ship terminals or to the mainland. As the dream of an "oil El Dorado" dominates the public mood on the island, the fate of its Native residents is given low priority. If new foreign-sponsored oil projects become reality, the results will be more resettlement of Native peoples, a high risk of sea pollution, and further appropriation of Native fishing and hunting lands.

Sakhalin's Native people are responding to the challenge by organizing their first political groups at village, district, and provincial levels. Their agenda focuses on issues of local self-government, protection of tribal lands, and state investment in Native educational, economic, and cultural programs.

For further reading, see: Black 1973; Ivanov, Levin, and Smolyak 1964b; and Watanabe 1972.

17

18

Ancestral Times

William W. Fitzhugh

Native American Origins

The evidence of early bone and stone tools suggests that the earliest cultures and peoples of the New World arrived from Asia at the end of the last Ice Age, about 12,000-15,000 years ago. Spreading rapidly in uninhabited territory where animals were plentiful and had little fear of humans, these early groups soon populated nearly the entire territory of the Americas, except for the arctic regions and Greenland, which were settled by a later wave of arctic-adapted Asian peoples about 4,000 years ago. By virtue of geography, Alaska and eastern Siberia played prominent roles in the history of Asian-American contacts and exchanges for more than 10,000 years.

When Europeans began to explore America, it was thought that Native Americans must have had European ancestry, but when Vitus Bering discovered Bering Strait in 1741, theories of Asian origins began to receive support. Today there are numerous theories about the peopling of the New World, but all of them acknowledge the importance of Siberia and Alaska in this process. One prominent current theory proposes three migrations of Asian peoples to account for patterns in Native American languages, gene pools, and archeological data. This theory holds that most of the peoples and cultures of the Americas originated in the earliest wave of Asian peoples, who arrived in Alaska over the Beringian land bridge, or along its Pacific coast, and spread south when glacial ice began to melt about 12,000-14,000 years ago. Archeological traces of these first Americans are seen in what archeologists call the Clovis culture, with its distinctive type of fluted point, a variety of which is known also in Alaska. To date, no known prototype for American Clovis culture has been found either in Asia or the Americas.

A second wave of Asian settlers left artifacts in a style called the Siberian-American Paleoarctic tradition. Sites of this tradition, which contain microblades, cores, bifaces, burins, and other specialized stone tools, are found on both sides of Bering Strait, at Ushki Lake (Figs. 19, 20), Diuktai, and other Siberian sites, and later, by 10,000 years ago, at Alaskan sites of the Denali culture (Fig. 22). Because Denali sites are limited to Alaska and the Northwest Coast, that culture may be the ancestor of modern Athapaskan and Tlingit peoples.

The third and final group of American cultures thought to have Asian connections are Eskimos and Aleuts. Early Eskimo-Aleut culture is believed to have appeared about 8,000 years ago in the Bering Sea and North Pacific region. Its earliest sites are found at Anangula and Ocean Bay, and its distinctive features include a focus on sea-mammal hunting using harpoons, kayaks, oil lamps, and other northern maritime adaptations. Although Eskimo-Aleut culture probably derived from earlier cultures of the area, the influence of Siberian Neolithic cultures was also important.

While this three-part theory accounts reasonably well for current knowledge, little is known for certain about the early history of the Americas, and of Siberia and Alaska in particular. The real prehistory of Beringia will not be known for decades or centuries and no doubt will be illuminated by Native oral history and tradition.

17.

Aleut figurines

Collected by M. Mangus in Port Moller, Alaska, 1981. National Museum of Natural History, Smithsonian Institution, #A492418 (left), 8.5 cm; A492416 (center), 9.3 cm; A492417 (right), 8.5 cm.

These remarkable ivory figurines were found at an archeological site in Port Moller, Alaska, but little is known of their original location, culture, or age. They are absolutely unique; their bold, stylized form is unlike any other prehistoric Eskimo or Aleut figurines. The central figure wears a bird or seal crest; the figure at right, a topknot. Facial features resemble Aleut and Pacific Yupik ceremonial masks. Limb joints are marked with lines, and collars or necklaces are shown. Grooved perforations on the backs facilitated mounting. They probably had religious significance and may depict deities or ancestors.

18.

Harpoon hunting magic

Old Bering Sea culture socketpiece found on St. Lawrence Island, Alaska, by E.D. Jones in 1936, dated ca. 1 B.C. to A.D. 500, National Museum of Natural History, Smithsonian Institution, #A378054. 21 cm.

This engraved socketpiece of fossilized walrus ivory, part of an Old Bering Sea culture harpoon, depicts a predator capturing its prey. This imagery—together with other engraved decorations, raised bosses, and drilled holes for mounting decorative bristles—illustrates an important aspect of early Eskimo hunting magic. By making beautiful weapons, hunters showed respect for animal spirits, which in turn offered themselves to the people and were received as "honored guests."

Beringia: The Asian-American Land Bridge

Scientists believe that people first moved into the Americas across the Beringian land bridge, or along its southern shores. This "land bridge" (actually the exposed sea floor of the Bering and Chukchi seas) today lies 50-100 meters (150-300 feet) underwater but existed as dry land at several periods during the last million years. In effect it was more like an extension of Asia than a "bridge," a vast expanse of tundra, almost 1,000 miles wide, connecting Asia and North America. This area was a productive habitat for arctic-adapted plants and animals, including caribou, mammoths, and other large game, and its southern coast was rich in marine mammals, fish, and seabirds. Once early Asian peoples mastered the basic techniques of arctic survival, probably 20,000-40,000 years ago, human expansion into Beringia and the later peopling of the New World was sure to follow.

The first route into the Americas has been debated for more than a century. These debates have been largely theoretical, because the archeological sites of these early migrants are now under water. Beringia probably reached its greatest extent 17,000-25,000 years

ago. As the Ice Age climate warmed, glacial ice melted and the sea level began rising. Bering Strait appeared about 11,000 years ago, and by 6,000 years ago the modern shorelines of Alaska and Siberia were established.

Through most of the glacial period, glaciers blocked access to the rest of North America. Ice covered the Brooks and Alaska ranges, and glaciers covering the Canadian Rockies merged with the Laurentide Ice Cap in eastern Canada to create a solid glacial mass from the Pacific to the Atlantic. But by 12,000-14,000 years ago, narrow channels began to open to the east and south, and ice-free corridors may have opened east of the Rockies and along the coast of Alaska and British Columbia. Through these corridors the first Asian migrants may have moved south into more temperate regions, discovering a vast, pristine, rich, uninhabited land. Within 1,000 years these "first Americans" expanded throughout North and South America. Only the Canadian arctic, covered by ice until 5,000 years ago, and Greenland remained unoccupied until Eskimo peoples expanded east from Alaska about 4,000 years ago.

19

19.

Early Ushki culture
(ca. 12,000 B.C.),
Kamchatka, Siberia
Collected by Nikolai Dikov.
Northeastern Interdisciplinary
Research Institute, Magadan,
Russia. Left to right (top to
bottom): bifacial knife blade
#YI-VII-30, 8.7 cm; stemmed
points, 2.8 cm, and #Ush-V-75,
2.7 cm; drilled stone beads;
three microblades, Y-414,
Y-I-410, and 409; and stemmed
point #Y-I-73-VII, 4.2 cm.

One of the earliest archeological
sites in the North Pacific region is

at Ushki Lake on the Kamchatka
River, where people began settling
to catch salmon. Over time their
camps were buried under volcanic
ash and silt, creating a deep strat-
ified record of successive cultures.
The earliest remains, dating to
12,000 B.C. (Level VII), include
outlines of skin tents and fireplaces
with bones of bison, horse, and
salmon. Level VII also
contained a human grave
covered with red ocher, and more
than 1,000 decorative ground-
stone beads.

20.

Late Ushki culture
(ca. 9000 B.C.),
Kamchatka, Siberia
Collected by Nikolai Dikov.
Northeastern Interdisciplinary
Research Institute, Magadan,
Russia. Left to right (top to bottom): leaf-shaped bifacial points
#Ush-I-IV DG, 9.3 cm; #Ush-80,
5 cm; #Ush-88, 3.9 cm; arrow (?)
point, 2.5 cm; round skin scraper,
2.2 cm; flake knife #Ush-82, 5.9
cm; two microblade cores #UI-VI-
22-Zh, 4.1 cm and 3 cm; and
two microblades, #U-VI-315.

3,000 years after the first occupa-
tion, people returned to Ushki
(Level VI) and built Eskimo-style
houses with central hearths and
subterranean entrance tunnels.
One house contained a dog burial
and a ritually scorched bison
shoulder blade. Late Ushki stone
tools include leaf-shaped bifaces
and projectile points, scrapers,
knives, and microblade technology.
Similarities to Siberian Diuktai
and American Denali culture sites
indicate that Late Ushki is part of
Siberian-American Paleoarctic
tradition.

20

21.

Paleoindian tradition

Three points from the National Museum of Natural History, Smithsonian institution. Top left, Clovis-like fluted point A391806 from Utokok River, Alaska, ca. 9000 B.C., 5.5 cm; bottom left Putu point SIC-200-1, Putu site, north Alaska, ca.8500 B.C., 2.3 cm; right, Healy Lake point, unnumbered, central Alaska, ca. 9000 B.C., 11.4 cm.

The oldest manmade objects in Alaska date to about 10,000 B.C. Their makers are called Paleoindians, the first inhabitants of North America. Unlike Denali culture (Fig. 22), Utokok, Healy Lake, and Putu points have no known links to Siberia.

22

22.

Denali culture

(ca. 8700-5200 B.C.) Dry Creek, Alaska. University of Alaska Museum. Left to right (top to bottom): two bifaces #UA77-44-3884, 12 cm, and UA74-41-199, 5 cm; two burins, UA77-44-370 and UA76-155-5496, 2.6 cm; two microblade cores DCr73-24, 3.2 cm, and DCr79-32, 4 cm; two microblades DCr73-47 and 48.

Among the earliest archeological sites in Alaska are small fishing and hunting camps on river terraces near Mount Denali. Denali tools include bifaces, stemmed points, burins, and microblades made from wedge-shaped cores. Denali sites date later than Siberian members of the Siberian-American Paleoarctic tradition, indicating eastward expansion of a tradition arising in Asia.

23.

Early maritime cultures in Alaska

Ocean Bay culture, 4000 B.C., from the KOD-363 site, Rice Ridge, Kodiak Island. Koniag, Inc., Kodiak, Alaska. Left to right: slotted bone shaft with microblades, #363-89-6-129-245, 10.8 cm, 363-89-372-2, 363-89-3-49-2, and 363-89-6-27-2; ivory throwing-board pin, 3.4 cm; and two harpoon heads #363-881-1-20-129, 9.3 cm, and #363-881-137-210, 9.8 cm.

Coastal sites in the Aleutians and on the Gulf of Alaska, 8,000-10,000 years old, indicate that

Siberian cultures quickly adapted to the rich supply of sea mammals, fish, and seabirds along Alaska's Pacific coast. At this time glacial ice still blocked sections of the coast. But even before 4000 B.C. maritime cultures like Ocean Bay I were using kayaks, harpoons, and throwing boards (note the tiny bone hook, which held a spear in place on a throwing board) to capture seals, sea lions, and sea otters, and smaller harpoons for fish and waterfowl. The use of slotted bone points with microblade insets ties Ocean Bay culture to earlier Siberian Paleolithic and Mesolithic traditions.

23

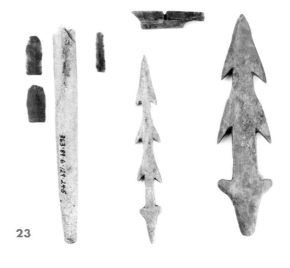

The Siberian Neolithic: Origins of Settled Village Life

With the onset of warming at the end of the Ice Ages, cultures of eastern Siberia, as in Pacific Alaska, began to specialize in sea and river hunting and fishing. Economies based on sea mammals, fish, and shellfish proved more stable than the previous land hunting economy, resulting in population growth and a settled way of life. Large coastal and riverine villages in Japan's Jomon and Russia's Lower Amur River sites indicate larger populations and increased sedentary life by 9,000-10,000 years ago, well before their appearance in Alaska. Most striking, however, is the presence of ceramic cooking vessels and clay animal figurines that were probably hunting charms. These ceramics are among the earliest in the world and indicate the potential of intensive fishing and maritime hunting economies for higher cultural development.

24.

Sakhalin Island Late Neolithic, Siberia

Sakhalin Regional Museum, Russia: four bone harpoon heads, from the Nevelsk II site, collected in 1957 by Kozyrev, left to right: #70-213, 7.5 cm, 70-219, 8.7 cm, 70-216, 9.3 cm, and 70-214, 11.5 cm; three arrowheads, from the Imchin II site, northern Sakhalin, #3753-153, 2.4 cm, #3753-74, 5.2 cm, and 3753-189, 3.5 cm; scraper #3753-215, from Imchin II, 6.2 cm; microblade core #3760-497, and two microblades #4516-14 and 4516-10, from Imchin II; two pottery sherds, left #4334-752, from the Sadovnik II site, southern Sakhalin, and right, #4720-3811, from the Imchin II site, northern Sakhalin, 10 cm and 11.5 cm.

By Late Neolithic times, ca. 3000-1000 B.C., Sakhalin Island cultures had toggling harpoons, ceramics, and an array of stone scrapers, knives, points, and microblades. By this time the distinctive features of coastal Siberian Neolithic, seen here in a collection from the Nevelsk II site, are fully developed. The variety of harpoon types indicates the evolution of harpoon technology. Hunters seem to have used decoration as hunting magic to please the spirits of prey and increase their success. Similar beliefs and practices are found among Alaskan Eskimo cultures.

25.

"Nefertiti" of the Amur, Siberia (cast)

Original at the Museum of History and Culture of the Peoples of Siberia and the Far East, Novosibirsk, Russia, #KN-63-48090. 11 cm. Excavations at the Kondon site in the lower Amur River recovered this remarkable fired clay figurine from a Neolithic dwelling dating to 4000-2000 B.C. An armless bust with a flat, swept-back forehead and carefully modeled facial features, the Kondon figurine may have served as a sevon (shaman's helper or guardian used to ward off disease) or dzhulin (female household deity or guardian).

The form resembles Alaskan Eskimo, Aleut, and Indian figurines that were used both as children's dolls and as charms and religious icons.

24

25

26.

Tarinski culture (3000-1000 B.C.), southern Kamchatka, Siberia

Kamchatka Regional Museum, Russia, left to right, top row: arrow head #29864-A5/310, 6.2 cm, Bol'shoi Kamen' site; bone tool #29925-A9/106, 7.8 cm; slate labret #GI-30283, 5.8 cm, Jupanovo site; human figure #GI-30282, 3 cm, Bol'shoi Kamen' site; two obsidian arrowheads #29864-A5/316, 2.2 cm, and #29864-A5/353, 2.8 cm; below, round scraper #29925-A9/89, 3 cm; bone pin or creaser #29925-A9/654, 9.4 cm; gray stone scraper 29864-A5/573, 6.4 cm; obsidian point #29864-A5/372, 4 cm; below, two obsidian scrapers #29925-A9/565, 3.2 cm and #29925-A9/31, 4.9 cm, mouth of the Riabukhina River; and engraved bone pendant #29925-A9/136, 10 cm.

The Tarinski culture of Kamchatka exhibits features common to other Late Neolithic Siberian cultures, such as Taria, Northern Chukotka, Ymyiakhtakh, and Ust'-Belaia. Other elements, such as labrets, indicate contacts with the wider North Pacific region. Labrets, T-shaped or plug-like ornaments worn in a hole in the lip, are found in most North Pacific cultures of this period. Tarinski materials also include chipped stone projectile points and asymmetric knives made of colorful chert; T-shaped scrapers; bone spatulas, pins, and creasers for crimping boot soles; and stone adzes and gouges for woodworking and boat building. Human figures of chipped stone probably represented spirit guardians used as hunting magic and protective devices. Such figures are found in many Siberian sites of this and later periods and are known in Alaskan Eskimo and Canadian Dorset culture.

27.

Tokarevski culture (1500-1 B.C.), northern Okhotsk Sea, Siberia

Kamchatka Regional Museum, Russia, left to right: two bone harpoons #cp-88 dz-1530, 10.5 cm, and #OL-83 N-35, 7.5 cm; two stone points #VX-1219-CP-89-d-14-25, 6.5 cm cm, and VX-1218-CP-V11-84g, 8 cm; below, two bone spear prongs #M-37 OL-87-20, 15.5 cm, and #OL-83-P-37, 20 cm.

Tokarevski culture is known from excavations in the Magadan region of the Okhotsk Sea. Like the Bering Sea, the Okhotsk is seasonally covered with pack ice and is one of the richest marine habitats of the North Pacific. Protected from the open ocean and fed by nutrients from the Amur River, the Okhotsk Sea nurtured the development of highly complex prehistoric cultures. Tokarevski culture closely parallels the development of Eskimo and Aleut cultures in its economy, dwelling types, village life, and technology. The latter included fixed and detachable harpoons, and trident spears for birds and fish. Many of the harpoon forms show close stylistic parallels with early Eskimo harpoons from the Bering Sea, but lack the ornamentation of early Eskimo and Aleut cultures.

26

27

28.

Tokarevski stone pendants, northern Okhotsk Sea, Siberia (1500-1 B.C.)

Kamchatka Regional Museum, Russia, left to right: #VX-1224, 2.7 cm, ; #VX-1228, 4.1 cm; #VX-1227, 3.3 cm; #VX-1226, 3.6 cm; #VX-1225, 6 cm.

An exceptional feature of Tokarevski culture is its use of ground stone pendants for ritual charms and protective devices. Pendant forms include human and animal shapes and oval discs incised with skeletal patterns. Many display notched edges. These pendants probably served as personal guardians. A number of cultures in the North Pacific and arctic regions use pendant charms that feature skeletal patterns, animal images, and notched edges.

28

Development of Northern Maritime Societies

During the past 6,000-8,000 years, peoples living along the shores of the North Pacific and Bering Sea learned to adapt their technology and cultures to the rigorous climate, environment, and animals of this northern maritime region. This process, epitomized by the Eskimo-Aleut type of culture, included development of special technology and skills for hunting marine mammals with skin kayaks, harpoons, throwing boards, and multi-pronged bird and fish spears; warm tailored skin garments; semi-subterranean dwellings heated by blubber- and oil-fueled lamps; and special tools such as boot-creasers, ulus, needle cases, and others. This process is most dramatically noted in the development of North Alaskan Eskimo culture; more generalized northern maritime forms appear among peoples of the Okhotsk Sea, the Aleutian Islands, and the Pacific coast of Alaska and the Northwest Coast. While the roots of this adaptation to northern maritime settings began in the Siberian Paleolithic and was pioneered by the earliest Alaskan peoples, it is most notable among later cultures where bone, ivory, and other organic materials have been preserved. Siberian and Alaskan/Northwest Coast cultures began to exhibit these tendencies simultaneously about 4000-5000 B.C. New inventions and skills spread so quickly through a chain of maritime-based societies across thousands of miles, that today it is difficult to tell how and where these developments first occurred.

29.

Denbigh and the Arctic Small Tool tradition (2500-1500 B.C.), Alaska

University of Alaska Museum, Fairbanks, left to right (top to bottom): three endblades #IYEB6-8, 3.5 cm; UA64-99-9, 3.4 cm; and #CS-66-2700, 7.7 cm; two bone harpoon heads, #UA68-62-322, 10.3 cm, and #UA68-62-260, 9.6 cm, from the Denbigh site; black chert projectile point #CS-354, 6.5 cm, from the Campus site; Denbigh grey chert borer #UA64-99-46, 5.2 cm; Denbigh mitt-shaped grey chert burin #UA64-99-108, 2.5 cm; below left: mitt-shaped brown chert flake knife #UA64-99-25, 4 cm; black chert side blade #UA64-99-67, 4.7 cm; and grey chert end scraper #UA64-99-42, 2.7 cm, from the Denbigh site; brown chert microblade core from the Campus site #CS-3-16, 3.6 cm.

In the early 1960s archeologists working at Cape Denbigh in Norton Sound discovered a new arctic culture, the Denbigh Flint Complex. This culture left behind delicately flaked flint points, knives, perforators, skin scrapers, microblades struck from wedge-shaped cores, and burins, a special class of tool used for grooving bone, antler, ivory, and wood. The burins, microblades, and the delicate flaking styles of these tools were nearly identical to those found in late Neolithic cultures in northern Yakutia and Chukotka. Denbigh lacked only the pottery found in these Siberian sites. Instead of mounting microblades in slotted points, the Denbigh culture used crescent-shaped bifacial sideblades, which produced a stronger cutting edge.

Denbigh harpoons did not toggle but had detachable points with restraining lines. Small fixed harpoons were used for birds and fish.

The early Ocean Bay cultures of Kodiak Island used similar harpoons with bilateral barbs (see Fig. 23).

Denbigh people had great appreciation for fine flint-working techniques. Their tools are beautifully crafted from multicolored chert, chalcedony, and other glass-like rocks. "Ripple" flaking, a fine art in itself, ensured that a hunter's tools would glitter, thus pleasing and attracting animal spirits.

Denbigh culture was succeeded in western Alaska by Norton culture (small points at left), which retained Denbigh's flint-working traditions and added stone grinding and Siberian-derived ceramics to its technology, and semi-subterranean dwellings to its settlements. The latter indicates increased sedentary life as a result of a more productive arctic maritime economy.

It is thought that Denbigh culture is part of a larger entity known to archeologists as the Arctic Small Tool tradition (ASTt), which originated from developments within Siberian Neolithic cultures about 3000 B.C. Denbigh brought new changes and perhaps new people into the Bering Strait region. A refined version of early arctic interior hunting and fishing cultures, the ASTt quickly became established in Alaska and spread, within a few centuries, south along the Bering Sea coast to the Alaska Peninsula. Moving east, they pioneered human settlement in the Canadian Arctic (only recently free of glacial ice), Greenland, and Labrador. In the process ASTt cultures learned to exploit seal and other marine animals, but they never became proficient hunters of large marine mammals, perhaps because they lacked efficient toggling harpoons.

29

Harpoons and Northern Sea-Mammal Hunting

Developments in harpoon technology resulted in a major breakthrough in the hunting of large marine mammals in the northern oceans, especially in ice-covered seas. For thousands of years peoples all over the world—as early as 40,000 years ago in the rivers and lakes of East Africa—used barbed harpoons to capture large fish for which hooks were too weak and inefficient. Whether fixed onto shafts, detachable, or equipped with restraining lines, harpoons were important implements of Paleolithic hunters and were used for both land and marine game.

On the northern sea coasts, harpoons were indispensable in capturing sea mammals, but they remained relatively inefficient until the invention of the toggling harpoon. Upon striking prey, a toggling harpoon detaches from its shaft, turns, and sticks beneath the skin and blubber of the animal. Lines from the harpoon let the hunter tire his prey and eventually dispatch it with spear or club. While this technique worked well from boats, the toggling harpoon had its greatest impact along coasts where pack ice forms in winter, for here hunters could exploit an ecosystem previously unavailable to man. Ultimately this led to an explosion of arctic coastal hunting cultures as Eskimo peoples expanded north from the Bering Sea into northern Chukotka, Alaska, Canada, and Greenland.

Archeologists believe the toggling harpoon was invented about 6,000 to 7,000 years ago, but its place of origin is still unclear. Toggling harpoons appeared in the North Pacific around 4,000 years ago, in the later stages of the Arctic Small Tool tradition in Denbigh culture and its Canadian equivalent, Pre-Dorset culture. However, the earliest toggling harpoon known in North America was found in early Maritime Archaic Indian cultures of subarctic Newfoundland and Labrador, 5,000 miles from Bering Strait, dating around 7,000 years ago. Since the first Denbigh/ ASTt people who entered the Canadian Arctic had simple barbed harpoons (similar to those in Fig. 29), toggling harpoons may have been borrowed by Pre-Dorset people in contact with Maritime Archaic Indians in Labrador about 4,000 years ago. Shortly after, small Maritime Archaic-type toggling harpoons appeared in ASTt cultures in Canada and Alaska, where they became common among the earliest true arctic maritime culture to adapt fully to the arctic coasts and islands of the Chukchi Sea. This culture, known as Old Whaling, hunted seals, small whales, walrus, and polar bear, and is found in northwest Alaska and on Wrangel Island, 200 miles north of Chukotka.

It remains to be seen whether early Asian cultures participated in the development of toggling harpoons. Similar harpoons are known from Jomon culture sites in Japan dating as early as 6,000 years ago. However, it is not clear that these forms led to the complex toggling harpoons of later Jomon or were part of Bering Sea developments. The dating of Late Neolithic harpoons in the Russian Far East, on Sakhalin Island (Fig. 24), and elsewhere is still uncertain. But after 2000 B.C. virtually all coastal cultures of the North Pacific and Bering and Chukchi seas had access to this technology. In the succeeding two millennia, refinements in toggling harpoons, the addition of restraining floats, and the development of open boats with whaling crews permitted peoples north of the Aleutian Islands to hunt large whales. This development, which may have had an important Siberian component, produced a major cultural revolution among northern Bering Sea cultures after A.D. 500.

30.

Old Koryak bone harpoons (ca. A.D. 1000) from northern Kamchatka, *collected by A.K. Ponomarenko's team, Kamchatka Regional Museum, Russia, left to right: barbed harpoon #29726-A4/549, 11.5 cm; toggling harpoon #29726-A4/542 (head pin), #29726-A4/541 (head), and #29726-A4/540 (blade); and toggling harpoon with asymmetrical barbs #29726 A4/550, 6.5 cm.*

The ancestor of Koryak culture of the northern Okhotsk Sea and Kamchatka is known as Old Koryak culture. Like Old Kerek to the north, Old Koryak has a strong Eskimo "flavor" in its bone and ivory technology. The seal harpoons illustrated here include toggling forms with round shaft sockets and barbed blades (left). At center is a complete "Eskimo type" toggling harpoon assembly with foreshaft, harpoon head (with hole for the retrieving line), and chert endblade.

The sealing harpoon head at right is particularly interesting; its barbs resemble metal arrowpoints found in Iron Age sites in the Amur Basin to the south.

30

The Rise of Eskimo Cultures

One of the most dramatic developments in the prehistory of the North Pacific was the development of Eskimo cultures. Eskimo culture is thought to have originated in the Bering Sea region through a process of local cultural development and interaction with other cultures of the Pacific Coast, Aleutian Islands, and Siberia, a process that occurred over thousands of years. By at least 6,000 years ago, a distinct Eskimo/ Aleut language was in place among peoples of the southern Bering Sea.

Little is known of the first 4,000 years of this development because most Bering Sea sites of this period were submerged by rising seas. But by 2,500 years ago, a series of early Eskimo cultures known as Okvik, Old Bering Sea, and Ipiutak appeared in fully developed form in Bering Strait and northwest Alaska while, to the south, Norton culture exhibited strong Eskimo cultural identity as well. Eskimo-like cultures also appeared in Chukotka and northern Kamchatka at this time. The features of these early Eskimo cultures include intensive use of sea mammals, relatively permanent village settlements with semi-subterranean dwellings, toggling harpoon technology, skin boats, blubber oil lamps, and distinctive religion, mythology, and art styles combining hunting magic with engraved and sculptural art. Many of these traditions can be traced from these early Eskimo cultures into the historic period, a remarkable history of cultural continuity linked to a single ethnic group or closely related series of groups.

Okvik, Old Bering Sea, and Ipiutak peoples overlapped in time and must have known each other. These early cultures each had distinctive artistic designs and styles of harpoons, which must have developed in part to mark hunting territories and social space. When elaborately decorated artifacts were buried as grave goods, these identities were also conveyed to the afterworld.

31.

Eskimo cultures of Bering Strait Harpoons from St. Lawrence Island, Alaska

Left to right: Ipiutak Eskimo culture bone harpoon with stone side blades, collected by H.B. Collins in 1921, dated ca. 1 B.C. to A.D. 500, National Museum of Natural History, Smithsonian Institution, #A346914, 10 cm; Early Punuk Eskimo culture ivory harpoon collected by H.B. Collins in 1929, dated ca. A.D. 500, National Museum of Natural History, Smithsonian Institution, #A346907, 10.2 cm; Old Bering Sea Eskimo culture ivory harpoon collected by H.B. Collins in 1931, dated ca. 500 B.C., National Museum of Natural History, Smithsonian Institution, #A353767, 13 cm; Late Punuk Eskimo culture ivory harpoon, dated ca. A.D. 1000, University of Alaska Museum, Fairbanks, #UA85-150-1261, 8.4 cm; and below: Thule Eskimo culture bone and stone arrow head collected by Chambers in 1933, dated ca. 1200, National Museum of Natural History, Smithsonian Institution, #A346907, 17.7 cm.

The early Eskimo cultures of Bering Strait and north Alaska are recognized by the distinctive styles, shapes, and decoration of their tools—in this case a group of harpoon heads. From left: The Ipiutak harpoon head has multiple spurs and side-blades. The early Punuk head is decorated with incised lines and drilled holes that may once have held seal bristles. The "feather"-spurred Old Bering Sea head is carved as a bird of prey. The Late Punuk head illustrates the simplification of hunting technology among the Inupiaq north of Bering Strait after A.D. 1000. Among Yupik people to the south, artistic treatment of harpoon heads was retained until the historical period. A bone-mounted arrowhead is also illustrated.

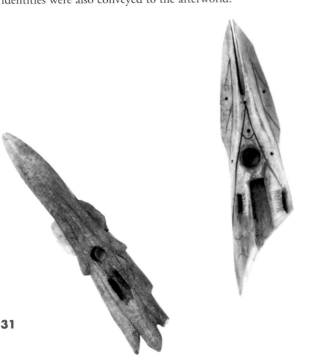

31

Contacts, Trade, and War

By about A.D. 500 most of the fine flint-working technology of the Late Neolithic period in northeastern Siberia and western Alaska had been replaced by metal or ground slate blades and bone and ivory tools, as these cultures and early Eskimo cultures of Bering Strait became familiar with metal through trade with iron-using peoples to the west and south.

The first evidence of iron among the cultures of Bering Strait and northwest Alaska are found in the Old Bering Sea and Ipiutak cultures, where iron tips were used on drills and delicate engraving tools. Even when iron or bronze was not available directly, knowledge of metalwork is seen in ivory imitations of metal chains used on ritual drinking vessels, and in the bone imitations of metal ornaments that decorated Siberian shaman's coats.

In exchange for metal (and later during the historic period for glass beads, tobacco, and manufactured products supplied across Bering Strait through Russian-Chukchi-Eskimo trade systems) Alaskan Eskimos supplied furs, jade, finished wood products, and other commodities to their Asian counterparts. These exchanges took place at annual trade fairs that attracted large numbers of people from throughout western Alaska. Many Asian products eventually reached Canadian Eskimo and Alaskan Indian and Aleut peoples through the rapidly expanding trade networks that developed during the past 3,000 years across Bering Strait.

In addition to economic exchanges, contacts across Bering Strait and with other regions of Alaska and Canada promoted major social and political changes. As populations grew and diversified as a result of increasingly efficient local hunting and fishing economies, Alaskan and Siberian societies began to experience stress and competition for resources and access to trade goods. The result is particularly evident after A.D. 500 when slat armor, sinew-backed bows, and other elements of war technology seem to have been introduced into Alaska from Siberia. Raiding and warring across Bering Strait and along the coasts of Alaska to acquire goods, slaves, and prestige became a common occurrence during the past 1,000 years, resulting in fortified refuges, the appointment of war captains, new social and political hierarchies, and the spread of new technologies.

These patterns were established long before Europeans entered the region. Rather than increasing the levels of violence, the appearance of Europeans—first Russians and later Euroamericans—appears to have caused its decline. But while inter-cultural warfare may have declined when Native peoples found they could acquire trade goods directly from Europeans, the saving in lives was far offset by death from introduced European diseases and other factors.

32.

Barbed Aleut harpoon (ca. A.D. 1000)

National Museum of Natural History, Smithsonian Institution, #A395958, 23.6 cm. Prehistoric Aleut groups used elaborate barbed harpoons to capture sea lions, seals, and possibly even whales. When hunting whales, they anointed harpoons with a poison made from aconite and the dried mummies of whalers. Aleut harpoons were very long and made from whale rib. This harpoon has a socket for a stone endblade. The three parallel lines below the socket are probably the hunter's mark, which allowed him to be credited with the kill should his wounded prey escape and be captured by another hunter. The distinctive pattern of barbs may have served the same purpose.

32

Sakhalin Island's Okhotsk Culture (A.D. 500-1500)

Late prehistoric Okhotsk Sea cultures flourished in the southern Okhotsk Sea region, living in large settled villages in deep, well-insulated pithouses. They hunted seals, sea lions, and birds, and collected seaweed and shellfish; land game included bears, pigs, and small animals. Okhotsk culture people lived as hunters and gatherers on the fringe of rice-farming and pig-breeding societies in Japan and China, and they also had contacts with Kamchatkan hunters and reindeer herders. They knew metal, but it was an expensive and rare trade item, and their tools were largely of stone. Pottery was widespread, decorated with stamped impressions of bear tracks, dogs, foxes, geese, and other animals. These images probably honored the spirits of these useful creatures and served in part as hunting charms.

33.

Okhotsk culture pottery sherds (ca. A.D. 500)

Sakhalin Regional Museum, Russia. Sherds depicting [8843] bat or seagull (?) #3757-2138, 5 cm; [8845] goose #3757-2156, 11 cm; [8842] bear #739-16, 3.7 cm; [8846] dog #3761-2481, 5.5 cm; [8844] bear paw #739-13, 4.3 cm; and [8841] fox #3761-1769, 3.5 cm. From the Ust'-Tunaicha, Ozerk I, Promyslovoe site, on southern Sakhalin Island.

33

34

34.

Bear head

Pumice bear head, from the Utesnaia I site, southern Sakhalin Island, about A.D. 1000. Sakhalin Regional Museum, Russia, #3756-49. 9 cm.

Bear rituals must have been an important part of Okhotsk religious life, for carvings of bears have been found in these sites. Okhotsk people probably captured young bears, reared them, and ritually killed and ate them, just as the Ainu people of this region have done in the historical era.

35.

Southern Sakhalin Island

Left to right, top row: two small bone harpoons #5081-19 and #5081-21, from Solov'evka, ca. A.D. 1000-1500, 5.2 cm and 5 cm; two toggling harpoons #5395-1011 and #5395-1553, from the Promyslovoe II site, 9 cm and 7 cm; bone harpoon #5082-2, from the Promyslovoe II site, and stone point 5081-14 from Solov'evka, 5.5 cm and 2.6 cm; stone point #5081-12, from Solov'evka. 5 cm. Bottom row: two stone arrow heads, 5081-13 and 5081-11, from Solov'evka, 3.5 cm and 4.1 cm; bone seal figure #5082-1, from the Promyslovoe II site, 4 cm; clay figure of a killer whale #3756-50, from the Utesnaia I site, 4.3 cm; knife blade #5081-9, from Solov'evka, 7.5 cm.

Okhotsk culture harpoons, made of bone, are often highly complex artistic creations, vaguely animal in shape or perhaps representing insects or beasts with spiritual connotations. Small harpoons for spearing fish did not require decoration, for the spirits of these animals were not considered as powerful and as difficult to capture.

35

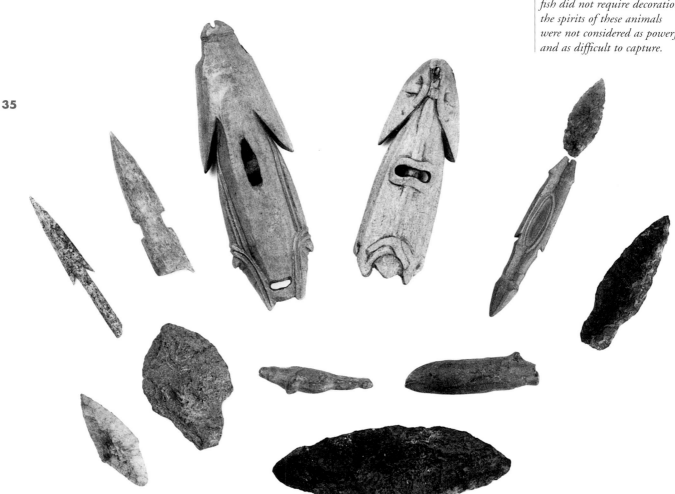

Crossroads Times

Valérie Chaussonnet

Home is not just a wooden or skin structure, not just a house or village. It is a feeling of familiarity, a combination of smells, tastes, sounds, images, and warmth.

36.

Koryak winter scene. Maritime village at the turn of the century. Koryak houses were octagonal, built partially underground. A "storm roof" like an inverted cone kept snow from covering the dwelling and served as a storage area and workplace in good weather. W. Jochelson, Spring 1901. Jesup Expedition. American Museum of Natural History neg. #4123.

Home

Home is a way of doing things, the look of a dwelling, the sound of one's mother-tongue—all the things that make up the social language of the culture. Home represents shelter, not only from the elements, but also from the power of evil spiritual forces. Therefore, charms and house guardians are as important to a home as the lamp, the hearth, and the sleeping platform.

In their structure and placement of furniture, Alaskan and Siberian family houses reflect a culture's notions of status and gender divisions, of relationships to animals, spirits, and the creation of art. Construction and use of the home follow rules and taboos that make the home a strong habitat, a sound shelter from dark forces, and an image of balance and rightness.

From hide-covered summer tents to semi-underground winter dwellings, the wide variety of local styles demonstrates great ingenuity in the use of local resources and materials and in adaptation to climate or to the demands of a nomadic life. Some Native types of dwellings (somewhat modernized) are still in use today, mainly temporary structures used during summer camps and hunting trips. Others, such as semi-subterranean wooden houses, have been totally replaced—but often the new houses still contain traditional divisions of space.

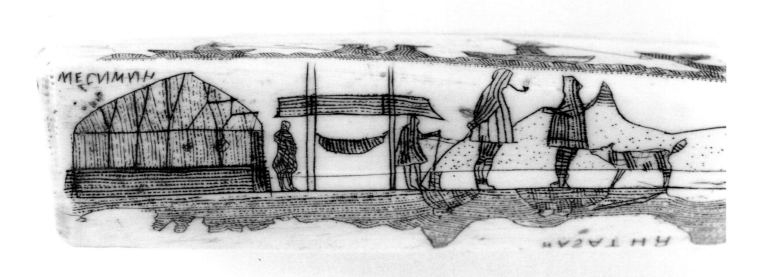

37.

Village in Chukotka

Detail from walrus tusk carving, collected in 1948. Vladivostok Maritime Museum, Russia, #2688. 16 cm.
Village scene at Mechigmen (the artist wrote Mesimin), a formerly Asian Eskimo then Chukchi community in the vicinity of Lorino which was deserted early this century, with baidara drying upside down on its rack, a *skin iaranga whose skin cover is held down with stones and ropes, and men smoking and chatting in gutskin parkas.*
The other side of the tusk features walruses and the name Iantagai, another village in the same area now called Iandogai.

38.

Women's corner
Koniag wooden grease bowl, and wooden handle with carved puffins, from the KAR-001 site on Kodiak Island, Alaska, A.D. 1400, both from Kodiak Area Native Association collections. Bowl unnumbered, 14.2 cm; handle #UA83-193-1804, 15.8 cm.

Three miniature stone oil lamps, models or girls' toys, from left to right:

Ocean Bay I culture sandstone oil lamp from the KOD-363 site on Kodiak Island, Alaska, 4000 B.C. Kodiak Area Native Association, #363-90-10-84-18. 7.2 cm;

Koniag oil lamp from Kodiak Island, Alaska, A.D. 1400, collected in 1932 by Ales Hrdlicka. National Museum of Natural History, Smithsonian Institution, #A365544. 4.3 cm;

Inupiaq steatite oil lamp from Point Hope, Alaska, early 1900s. National Museum of the American Indian, #12/6807. 10.5 cm.

Used to light the home, dry clothes hanging above them on a rack, and boil food, oil lamps are the property of women and the essential piece of furniture in the Eskimo and Aleut house. They truly are, as Molly Lee puts it, the "cornerstone of life" (n.d.:10).

The soot from the lamp is used to make tatoos on women's chins, as a fertility charm, and on the cheeks, hands, arms, and thighs.

The grease saved in the Koniag wooden bowl was used as food and as fuel for the lamps. The bowl's elegant shape reminds one of a canoe.

39.

Home guardian

Koryak house guardian and fire board from Kamchatka, Siberia, about 1950, made of wood with dark pigment and leather. Kamchatka Regional Museum, Russia, #11174. 35 cm.

Fire boards and drills are used to light fires in the hearth. The Koryak and Chukchi consider the fire board a powerful guardian spirit of the house. A special ceremony is held as the first fire of the year is lit with the fire board, attended only by men, inside the chum. *The scratch marks around the mouth of this particular board testify that the spirit was fed grease or meat. The leather string was used to hang the board in the house.*

39

Men's workshop

Small box and men's working tools. Clockwise, from top:

Nivkh wooden drill haft from the village of Chir-Unvd, on Sakhalin Island, Siberia, late 1800s or early 1900s. Sakhalin Regional Museum, #2730. 31.3 cm. It was used in the fabrication of wooden objects. Its handle is ornate in the typical volute style of the Nivkh.

Yupik snuff box from Ukogumut, Alaska,1870s, made of ivory and wood with pigment. National Museum of Natural History, Smithsonian Institution, #E36252. 8 cm. Lid and bottom both bear the same red marking, possibly the mouth of a seal.

Nivkh knife from Sakhalin Island, Siberia, from the mid-1900s, made of carved wood and steel. Sakhalin Regional Museum, #3216-3. 23 cm.

Inupiaq flint flaker from Meade River (Atqasuk), Alaska, 1960, made of ivory, copper, sea mammal hide, and wood. University of Alaska Museum, Fairbanks, #UA64-21-479. 22.5 cm.

Bering Sea Eskimo ivory double-face drill handle collected in 1926 by Karl Lomen on Seward Peninsula, Alaska, dated from the 1800s. National Museum of Natural History, Smithsonian Institution, #A332197. 4.5 cm.

Chukchi bird-like drill handle made of bone, collected in 1927 by E.K. Fel'dman in Chukotka, Siberia. Vladivostok Maritime Museum, Russia, #647-61. 8 cm.

This drill handle was probably used to start fires, and the smiling bird is a reminder of the story that it was Raven who gave fire to men.

Prehistoric Eskimo knife from Point Hope, Alaska, made of antler and jade. University of Alaska Museum, Fairbanks, #1-1940-148. 10.5 cm.

Eskimo jadeite whetstone from Cape Prince of Wales, Alaska, collected in the 1800s by Mrs. Jeffery "from the Eskimo Kingegan." National Museum of the American Indian, #6/7881. 13 cm.

Prehistoric Eskimo drill and bit from Point Barrow, Alaska, made of antler and black chert. University of Alaska Museum, Fairbanks, #UA81-86-299. 5.3 cm.

Athapaskan gouge made by Jonas Robert, Venetie, Alaska, of wood, steel, screws. The point is made from a steel file. University of Alaska Museum, Fairbanks, #70-54-33. 16 cm.

Tlingit dragonfly awl from Southeast Alaska, collected in 1881 by J.J. McLean, made of mountain goat horn and metal. National Museum of Natural History, Smithsonian Institution, #E060133. 13.1 cm.

40

41

41.

Eskimo boxes: the realistic and the abstract

Realistic box in the shape of two seals, from Norton Sound, Alaska, collected in the 1870s by Lucien Turner, made of wood with pigment and glass beads. National Museum of Natural History, Smithsonian Institution, #E024346. 19 cm.

Abstract wooden box from an unknown provenience in Alaska, collected by Mrs. Thea Page in the 1800s. National Museum of the American Indian, #4/5203. 10.5 cm. Two crosses mark the ends of the box and lid where the faces of two animals, one on the back of the other, would be. The lid and body of the box are hinged together with a wooden peg.

The toys of Siberian and Alaskan children are often accurate miniature versions of objects from the adult world: tools and weapons for playing hunter, dolls to sew clothes for.

Doll-making has been practiced in the North Pacific since very ancient times. Archeologists have found 5,000-year-old ceramic dolls in the Amur River region—small human figures that were once clothed and probably served as amulets. Some ancient Eskimo dolls with movable arms and legs were probably inspired by Siberian examples. The Alaskan doll-making tradition—using wood, ivory, leather, grass, or paper—has developed from simple toys for children to modern collectors' items. Whereas Alaskan dolls are naturalistic, dolls from Siberia's Amur River region are almost abstract.

42.

Collector's doll
Yupik male doll in gutskin parka, made by Louise Toll from Hooper Bay, Alaska, of fabric, fur, gutskin, and beads. University of Alaska Museum, Fairbanks, #UA83-3-13. 30.5 cm.

42

43.

Dolls to play with

These three dolls were used as toys before they were collected. They were made for children, not for the collectors' market.

Athapaskan doll (center), collected by Lucien Turner in St. Michael, Alaska, in the1870s. It is made of wood, hair, beads, cotton, and leather. National Museum of Natural History, Smithsonian Institution, #E029766. 15.5 cm.

Two Yupik dolls collected in 1927 in Tanunak, Nelson Island. The feet on the small doll with bone head are made of caribou fur. Feet and hands on the taller doll are made of small rodent paws and fur held with grass. Note the tatooed lines on the chin of the wooden face, attributes of adult feminity in harmony with the female "frowning" mouth. A necklace of beads and a small metal bell hang from her neck as an amulet; originally, she was probably also wearing earrings. University of Alaska Museum, Fairbanks, #UA1084-10H (left) and #UA64-21-189 (right). 12 cm and 14 cm.

43

44

44.

Asian dolls for boys

Two Ulchi wooden dolls, hunters with braid, belt, and hunting bag, from the Amur river, Siberia, 1927. Khabarovsk Regional Museum, Russia, #1082 and #2183. 13.5 cm and 18 cm.

Nanai wooden stick dolls for boys called "buchukem", from the Amur River region:

back: 4 dolls from the early 1900s. Vladivostok Maritime Museum, Russia, #NV-766. 6.5 to14.8 cm. front: seven dolls made by A.A. Passar in 1991. Left to right: young man, hunter on skis, two dogs, tiger cub, little boy, and bear cub. Khabarovsk Regional Museum, Russia, #9735. 5 to 13.4 cm.

45.

Toys and games

From the top left:

Udegei wooden toy boat called ana *from the Amur River, Siberia, 1914. Khabarovsk Regional Museum, Russia, #2785. 12 cm.*

Two Yupik story knives, one old, one new, used by little girls to draw in the snow as they tell stories. The larger wooden knife was made in the 1940s or 1950s. University of Alaska Museum, Fairbanks, #UA67-98-285. 28 cm. The smaller ivory knife was collected on the Lower Yukon by Edward W. Nelson in the1870s. National Museum of Natural History, Smithsonian Institution, #E038537.

Nivkh toy wooden chain with bear heads from Sakhalin Island, Siberia, made in1990. Sakhalin Regional Museum, Russia, #528. 22 cm.

Two Athapaskan games: "Move the button over" yoke puzzle made by Isaac Tritt from Arctic Village, Alaska, in 1961, of wood, cotton string, plastic button; and ring and pin toy made by Abel Tritt from Arctic Village, Alaska, in 1970, of wood, cotton string, tanned caribou hide, and caribou tarsal bones. University of Alaska Museum, Fairbanks, #UA67-98-100 and #UA70-54-12. 18 cm and 17 cm.

Koniag ivory doll's head and jointed arm from Kodiak Island, Alaska, dated about A.D. 1400, collected in 1935 by Ales Hrdlicka. National Museum of Natural History, Smithsonian Institution, #A377654 (head), and # A377653 (arm). 4.5 cm and 6 cm.

Western Eskimo Thule Culture ivory doll from Cape Prince of Wales, Alaska, dated about A.D. 1000, collected in 1929 by Henry B. Collins. National Museum of Natural History, Smithsonian Institution, #A344639. 6.2 cm.

46.

Father and son
Inupiaq father and child collector's dolls made by Ethel Washington, Alaska, in the 1930s (?). The heads are carved in wood. National Museum of Natural History, Smithsonian Institution, unnumbered. 29 cm and 11 cm.

47.

Elegant paper dolls
Ulchi Khaka dolls made from paper, yarn, and fabric, by G. Kuisali, Amur River, Siberia, 1991. The body with the head is inserted into a slit in the dress at the neck. Khabarovsk Regional Museum, Russia, #VX3/14, 15, and 16. 12 cm.

48.

Noisy toys

From the top right to bottom:

Yupik rattling leather ball from St. Lawrence Island, Alaska, made of dyed (red) and bleached sealskin, caribou hair, and rattle. University of Alaska Museum, Fairbanks, #UA67-98-256. 12.5 cm.

Nivkh rattle made of fishskin, wood, and rattle, from Sakhalin Island, 1960s. Sakhalin Regional Museum, Russia, #101. 12.5 cm.

Inupiaq "wolf scarer" (bull roarer) noisemaker made by Chester Seveck from Point Hope, Alaska, in 1966, of baleen with a nylon cord. University of Alaska Museum, Fairbanks, #UA66-4-2. 15 cm.

Nanai wooden cradle rattle for boys, from the Amur River, 1926. Khabarovsk Regional Museum, Russia, #1236 E-833. 12 cm (sticks).

48

49.

Two men chasing a giant goose

Koryak wooden toy from Siberia, from the late 1800s. National Museum of Natural History, Smithsonian Institution, #E175599. 16.2 cm.

49

50.

Miniature toys

Chukchi walrus ivory toys: ax, snow beater, 2 oars, 2 knives, and a spear, from Chukotka, collected in 1925 by Lupandin. Vladivostok Maritime Museum, Russia, #976. 4 to 8 cm.

50

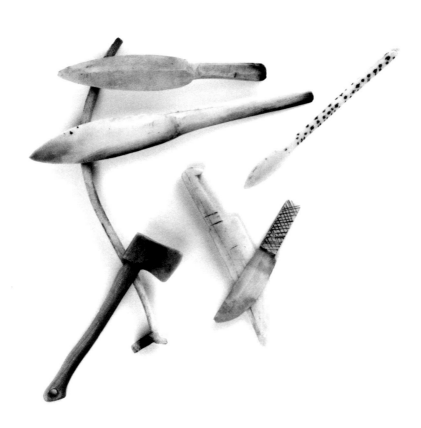

Fashion is a universal human passion that finds strong expression in Native Alaskan and northeastern Siberian cultures. This tradition is rich in face painting and tattooing, elaborate jewelry, beautiful fur garments, and embroidery.

Fashion

Dyed or processed fur and skins, dentalium shells, and, later, beads have been the object of active and passionate trade for centuries. Early western explorers commented on the stunning dress and look of Alaska's original inhabitants. Clothing, jewelry, and body ornaments identify one's ethnic group and social status, and also play the role of protective amulets.

In Siberia and Alaska, sewing is the specialty of women. The Tlingit Indians developed a unique tradition of weaving, and the seamstresses of the Amur became expert at sewing and embroidering fishskin to look like Chinese cotton and silk patterns. Because much of the work of piecing together animal skins, embroidery, and ornamentation has spiritual meaning, sewing is guided by numerous rules, like those governing men's hunting. Pouches made to hold sewing tools, thread, and sinew are often fine examples of the owner's skill in a variety of materials. Needles (originally made of bird bone), creasers, and other tools allow gifted seamstresses to do the fine stitching and embroidery that is the hallmark of North Pacific sewing.

51.

Koryak pouch
Koryak bird foot bag from Kamchatka, Siberia, about 1950, made of bird feet, reindeer fur, leather, and beads. Kamchatka Regional Museum, Russia, #11082. 26.5 cm.

52

52.

Small bag and ulus

Ulus are Eskimo women's knives. The round blade cuts skins and meat, for eating or sewing. The same smooth curve is found in the skirt of women's dresses and parkas, in sewing bags called housewives (see Fig. 53), and in women's oil lamps.

Yupik sealskin pouch from St. Lawrence Island, Alaska, collected by Farrar Burn,1800s. The white appliqué design and edges are bleached sealskin. National Museum of the American Indian, Smithsonian Institution, #11/6763. 13 cm.

From the top, a modern Yupik ulu made by Virginia Johnston from Bethel, Alaska, from moose antler and a steel blade. University of Alaska Museum, Fairbanks, #UA91-9-12. 6.5 cm.

Two prehistoric ulus from Point Hope, Alaska, made of old ivory and slate, and baleen and slate. University of Alaska Museum, Fairbanks, #1-1940-045 and #1-1940-046. 7.4 cm and 9.7 cm.

Toy Inupiaq ulu from Point Barrow, Alaska, made of new ivory (handle), and old ivory (blade), collected by J. E. Stanley. National Museum of the American Indian, Smithsonian Institution, #5/4578. 5 cm.

53.

Sewing bags

Orok embroidered bag from central Sakhalin Island, 1900-50, made of buckskin and cotton embroidery floss. Sakhalin Regional Museum, Russia, #2338-5. 12.7 cm.

Yupik fur "housewife" made of caribou fur, yarn, leather, and an ivory fastener, collected in 1886 by I. Applegate in Togiakumute, Alaska. Small tools were kept in the bottom pocket, the body of the bag was rolled around it, and it was finally secured with the ivory fastener. National Museum of Natural History, Smithsonian Institution, #E127354. 15 cm.

Aleut gutskin pouch made of seal gut, feathers, yarn, and cotton floss, and collected in 1931 by Mrs. Edward C. Robinson. National Museum of Natural History, Smithsonian Institution, #E362860. 14.5 cm.

53

Children's fashion

Koryak child's hat from Kamchatka, Siberia, about 1950, made of reindeer fur, otter fur, beads, leather, and plastic. The hat is zoomorphic, the two beaded disks on the side of the head imitating eyes and the fur attachments representing antler buds. It is made of two layers of fur for additional warmth and softness. Kamchatka Regional Museum, #23365. 22 cm.

Athapaskan child's bonnet from Venetie, Alaska, made in 1968 of pink felt, flannel, glass beads, and rabbit fur, with cloth ties. University of Alaska Museum, Fairbanks, #UA70-54-64. 19.2 cm.

Nanai child's fishskin mitts made in 1959 by Olga Samar from the village Nergem, Amur River region. Khabarovsk Regional Museum, Russia, #9502. 14 cm.

Nivkh mitt covers from Sakhalin Island made in the 1930s of fabric and cotton embroidery floss. Sakhalin Regional Museum, Russia, #1194-4. 22.4 cm.

54

Scraping skin

Koryak two-hand hide scraper and scraping board from Kamchatka, Siberia, about 1950, made of wood with a stone blade. The board is held vertically against the body to free the two hands for scraping downwards with the scraper. Kamchatka Regional Museum, #11278 (scraper), and #14340 (board). 51 cm and 42 cm.

Inupiaq hide scraper from Point Hope, Alaska, from the late 1800s, made of a wooden handle with baleen lashing around the chert blade. University of Alaska Museum, Fairbanks, #UA939/141. 9 cm.

Denbigh Culture black and grey chert scraper from Norton Sound, Alaska, dated about 1500 B.C. University of Alaska Museum, Fairbanks, #IYH1-D. 3.4 cm.

Nanai woman's knife and creaser called churuen, *used for skins and birch bark, from the village of Kondon on the Amur River, Siberia, dated from the 1950s, made of engraved wood with a small metal blade. Khabarovsk Regional Museum, Russia, #7753/3. 13.5 cm.*

55

56.

Koryak embroidery
Koryak embroidered band for use on clothing, made of leather, dark and white reindeer fur appliqué and slit embroidery, and silk and cotton threads. Kamchatka Regional Museum, Russia, #15577. 56.5 cm.

Koryak seamstresses are renowned for their virtuosity in embroidering various parts of clothing such as the opuvans, *the lower hem of their wide coats. Reindeer fur coats do not last more than one year, but the* opuvan *and other fancy parts of garments can be cut and recycled for the next season's clothing.*

57.

Koryak malakhai
Koryak adult man's hat called malakhai, *made after 1950 of two layers of reindeer fur for the winter, otter fur, dog fur, beads, leather, and plastic. Kamchatka Regional Museum, Russia, #28270. 28.5 cm.*

57

56

58.

Sewing tools

Prehistoric Eskimo ivory needle case from Point Barrow, Alaska. A strap of leather was used to wrap the fine bird bone needles in, then folded and kept inside the tube drilled in the needle case. Held vertically, this case shows two walrus snouts and tusks. University of Alaska Museum, Fairbanks, #UA-81-86-200. 11 cm.

Okvik culture (Eskimo) ulu handle in the shape of a vole-beast made of old ivory, collected in 1931 by Henry B. Collins on St. Lawrence Island, Alaska, dated about 1 A.D. National Museum of Natural History, Smithsonian Institution, #A352540. 8 cm.

Koryak bone thimble from Kamchatka, Siberia, about 1950. Kamchatka Regional Museum, Russia, #14353/E-685. 3.5 cm.

Prehistoric Eskimo ivory thimble holder from Point Hope, Alaska, and prehistoric Aleut bone needle or awl from Amaknak Island, Alaska. University of

Alaska Museum, Fairbanks, #1-1940-159 and #UA-68-62-71. 6.2 cm and 5.8 cm.

Thimble holders were attached with a leather strap to the end of the needle case, and themselves held a leather thimble. As with most Eskimo tools, they were often ornate and delicately engraved.

58

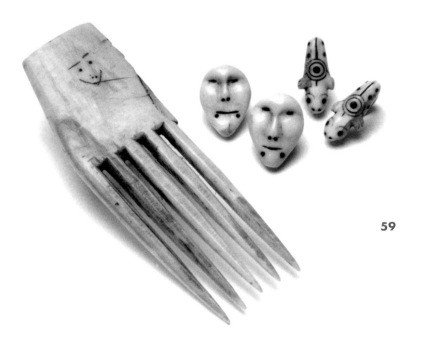

59

59.

Eskimo elegance

Prehistoric Eskimo ivory comb from St. Lawrence Island, Alaska. University of Alaska Museum, Fairbanks, #UA85-150-1246. 8.8 cm.

Yupik ivory earrings collected in Kushunuk, Alaska, in 1879 by Edward Nelson. The human faces wear labrets below the mouth. National Museum of Natural History, Smithsonian Institution, #E36859 and #E36860. 2 cm.

60

60.

Ornaments

This series is from the collection of the National Museum of Natural History, Smithsonian Institution.

Old Bering Sea culture (Eskimo) old ivory ornament and ivory disk from St. Lawrence Island, Alaska, dated at about A.D. 500, collected by Henry B. Collins in 1929 (ornament) and by Moreau Chambers in 1933 (disk). #A371923 and #A371841. 3.7 cm and 4.5 cm.

Western Thule culture (Eskimo) ivory woman with hair in bun, collected in Punuk Island, Alaska, by Henry B. Collins in 1929, dated at about A.D. 1000. #A342783. 3.7 cm.

Inupiaq blue bead labret collected by F.F. Fellows in Icy Cape, Alaska, from the 1800s. #E398256. 2.5 cm.

String of glass beads collected by Henry B. Collins in 1931 in Norton Sound, Alaska, from the 1800s. #A357008. 7 cm. Beads traveled a long distance from China or Venice before ending up on Alaskan labrets, amulets, jewelry, pouches, or clothes.

61

61.

Jet and baleen

Labrets, or lip plugs, are worn on the chin, at the corner of the mouth, or sometimes on the cheeks, by men and women among almost all Alaska Native cultures. The rules dictating who wears labrets and of what size and shape vary from group to group. It is an ancient practice which seems to have originated in Asia

(see Fig. 26 p. 41), and which purpose is aesthetic as well as magical and an affirmation of status.

Top: Inupiaq large baleen labret from Point Hope, Alaska, from the 1800s. University of Alaska Museum, Fairbanks, #UA1070. Young Inupiaq men wore small

labrets before being allowed to wear such a large size. The smooth flat part was inserted into the lip or cheek and rested against the gums.

Koniag jet and stone ornaments and labrets from Kodiak Island, Alaska, about A.D. 1400, collected by Ales Hrdlicka in 1935 and

1938. National Museum of Natural History, Smithsonian Institution, #A375350 (green labret), 5 cm, #A375703 (thin jet labret), 2.7 cm, #A395433 (jet bead), 3 cm, and #A395760 (jet whale tail ornament), 3 cm.

62.

Footwear

The variety of materials used for footwear illustrates the ingenuity, skill, and attention to detail that characterize North Pacific sewing as an art form. All are from the University of Alaska Museum, Fairbanks, collection.

From left to right:
Aleut child's boot from Unalaska, Alaska, made in1910-12 of sea lion throat. #UA77-32-7. 13.3 cm.

Athapaskan child's moccasin, made of commercially processed leather, rabbit fur, glass beads, cotton cord, and flannel lining. #UA89-13-6A. 10.4 cm.

Inupiaq doll's boot made in Candle, Seward Peninsula, Alaska, in 1946, of sealskin, caribou hide, and sinew. #UA86-8-9A. 9.7 cm.

Athapaskan child's cowhide boot, made of domestic calfskin, otter, felt, and leather ties. #UA88-13-3A. 13 cm. The use of calfskin is unusual.

The seamstress took advantage of the black and white natural pattern to make these boots striking.

Yupik doll's boot, made between 1920 and 1940 of fishskin, thread, leather, and cloth. #UA64-70-2C. 7 cm.

63

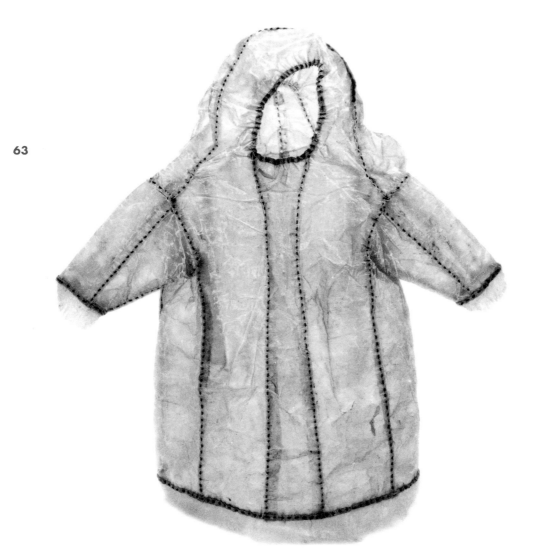

63.

Gutskin parka

Yupik doll's gutskin parka from Tanunak, Nelson Island, Alaska, made in 1926 of seal gut and thread. University of Alaska Museum, Fairbanks, #UA1084-7. 21.6 cm.

The guts are inflated, dried, then cut lengthwise and sewn with a special stiching so as to remain waterproof.

64.

Ball pincushion

Inupiaq pincushion made by Grace Bailey from Kotzebue, Alaska, in 1986, of bleached sealskin, leather, felt, sequins, and beads. University of Alaska Museum, Fairbanks, #UA86-13-26. 10 cm.

64

65.

Ainu elegance

Ainu woman's headband and glass beads from southern Sakhalin Island, late 1800s-early 1900s. The band is made of silk and cotton.Sakhalin Regional Museum, Russia, #85 - 5 and #58. 30 cm and 70 cm.

65

Spirits fill the world, and rocks, trees, and animals all live in human-like societies and behave like people. To understand the unknown, to cure illness, and to please the spirits of animals needed for food, spirits need to be honored with elaborate rituals and ceremonies.

Spirits

Charms and amulets are as fundamental as food and shelter to survival in a spirit-inhabited land. Small animal and human-like figures, strangely shaped pendants, carvings, and metal or bead attachments might be worn on clothing or against the skin to guard one's soul. Charms are attached to kayaks and equipment to insure a successful hunt.

Until recently, masks were used only for ceremonial purposes, such as dances, funerals, and other occasions. Masks might be realistic, fantastic, or abstract, but once a mask was put on, it changed the identity and the state of the wearer. In the same way, hats worn by dancers and shamans have fringes that conceal the wearer's face, signifying that a transformation is taking place. This rich masking tradition continues to inspire Native artists today.

66

66.

Masks that look like people

Inupiaq wooden female mask with tattoos from Point Hope, Alaska, from the late 1800s to the early 1900s, collected by Pedersen in 1929. National Museum of Natural History, Smithsonian Institution, #A348825. 22 cm.

Unlike most Yupik masks, fantastic or abstract (see Fig. 68), Inupiaq masks usually look realistically human. The painted hair is neatly combed, and the chin tattoos are a fertility charm.

Tlingit mask from the late 1800s, made of wood, pigment, and human hair. National Museum of Natural History, Smithsonian

Institution, #E073852-1. 20 cm. This mask is unusually small for a Tlingit mask. It displays an array of facial painting which a Tlingit man would wear for special occasions.

Prehistoric Eskimo stone pendant from Point Hope, Alaska. University of Alaska Museum, Fairbanks, #1-1940-152. 3.2 cm.

67.

Small faces

Tokarevski culture ivory pendant from Kamchatka, Siberia, dated 2000 to1000 B.C. Kamchatka Regional Museum, Russia, #VX-1223. 3.5 cm.

Prehistoric Eskimo old ivory doll head from Point Hope, Alaska. University of Alaska Museum, Fairbanks, #1-1940-033. 2 cm.

67

68.

Yupik faces

Concentric circle mask from Rasboinsky on the Yukon River, Alaska, and black and white mask from Pastolik, Alaska, collected by Edward W. Nelson in the 1870s. National Museum of Natural History, Smithsonian Institution, #E38862, 20.5 cm, and #E43770, 24 cm.

The concentric mask is one of a pair of almost identical masks. It originally had feathers around the top.

68

69.

Dancing finger mask

Yupik wooden finger mask from the Lower Kuskokwim River region, Alaska, collected by Edward W. Nelson in the 1870s. National Museum of Natural History, Smithsonian Institution, #E38649. 14 cm.

Dancers wear finger masks in pairs. This one originally had a series of feathers around it, which would bounce during the dance. It has two baby walrus tusks and a female "frowning" mouth, a symbol associated with sea mammals. The outer edge is painted red, showing the traditional Yupik lifeline.

69

70.

Siberian Eskimo faces

Two masks from the Big Diomede Island, Russia, collected by F.K. Gek in 1885. Vladivostok Maritime Museum, Russia, #1095-1 and #1095-2. 20 cm and 13.2 cm.

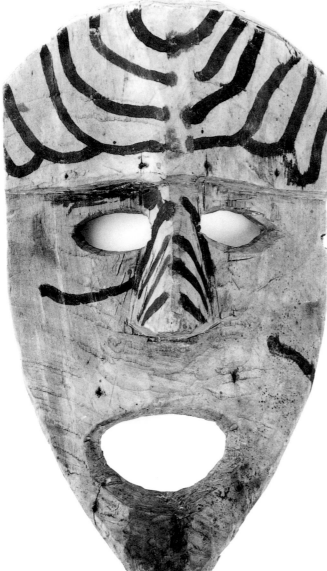

71.

Amur shaman's mask

Udegei Khambabo *(shaman)'s mask from the Amur River, Siberia, collected by V.K. Arsen'ev in 1911. Khabarovsk Regional Museum, Russia, #1608. 28.4 cm.*

71

72

72.

Snakes, fish, and beasts

Tlingit killer whale amulet from the late 1800s-early 1900s, and prehistoric Tlingit stone snake-beast with red pigments. National Museum of Natural History, Smithsonian Institution, #E229550 and #E067854. 16.5 cm and 4.5 cm.

Nanai Dadgifu, the spirit companion of Kalgama (see Fig. 75), collected in 1905 by B.O. Pilsudsky in the village of Troitskoe on the Amur River, Siberia. Vladivostok Maritime Museum, Russia, #2116-39. 15.3 cm.

Nanai bracelet with snake spirit made of fish skin sewn on fabric, from the Amur River, Siberia, collected in 1913 by I.A. Lopatin. Vladivostok Maritime Museum, Russia, #917-174. 24.5 cm.

73.

Transformations

Inupiaq ivory drum handle with walrus-man spirit from Point Barrow, Alaska, collected by P.H. Ray in 1881. National Museum of Natural History, Smithsonian Institution, #E56515. 12 cm. The face looks inside the drum, the drum frame resting on and being lashed to the "neck."

Nanai bear spirit made of wood and birch bark applique, from the Khabarovsk region, Siberia, 1992. National Museum of Natural History, Smithsonian Institution, unnumbered. 7 cm.

Ancestor-gods took the forms of bears to visit humans, and as such they are honored during the bear festival, now being revived in the Russian Far East.

Koniag human-raven transformation figure from Kodiak Island, Alaska, about A.D. 1400, made of wood. Koniag, Inc., Kodiak, #UA85-143-6888. 10 cm.

Two prehistoric Eskimo ivory bird-caribou amulets from St. Lawrence Island, Alaska. National Museum of Natural History, Smithsonian Institution, #A346407. 5.2 cm.

These compound creatures have ears and look like caribou crossing water, but the long beaks betray their transformational and spiritual nature.

73

74.

Magic pendants and skeletons

Objects that have magical properties often carry the outline of a skeleton, a sign of life and death, inside and outside nature, as well as of strength. Skeleton marks are found on early prehistoric Eskimo animal representations, such as in the Ipiutak culture. Holes, eyes, and circles, also of very ancient origin, are often conduits for the soul. Alaskan cultures have produced over the centuries countless small amulets, pendants, toggles, and objects bearing those magic signs. All

those shown here, except the Koniag wooden amulet, are from the National Museum of Natural History, Smithsonian Institution. From left to right:

Bering Sea Eskimo ivory animal pendant collected by Edward W. Nelson in Pastolik, Alaska, in 1878. #E33372. 7 cm.

Prehistoric ivory caribou hoof (?) pendant, and ivory figure with crest (?) from Uyak, both collected on Kodiak Island by Ales Hrdlicka in 1935 and 1938. #A377893 and #A395188. 6 cm and 7.5 cm.

Prehistoric St Lawrence Island Eskimo old ivory fox head pendant, collected by Ales Hrdlicka in 1937. #A390552. 2 cm.

Punuk (?) Eskimo culture long ivory pendant or ear ornament collected by Henry B. Collins on St. Lawrence Island, Alaska in 1931, dated at about A.D. 1000. #A356968. 5.4 cm.

Cottonwood bark Koniag multi-faced amulet from the KAR-001 site on Kodiak Island, Alaska, dated about A.D. 1400. Koniag, Inc., Kodiak, unnumbered. 8.4 cm.

Prehistoric Aleut ivory seal toggle from Attu Island, and ivory bear-whale amulet from Moknak, both collected by Ales Hrdlicka in 1937 and 1938. #A386269 and #A395757. 6 cm and 8 cm.

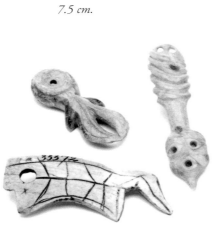

75.

Wooden sevens (spirits) and shaman

From left to right:

Nanai healing spirit, collected in 1904 by K.D. Loginovskii in the village of Troitskoe, on the Amur River. Vladivostok Maritime Museum, Russia, #2146-2. 23.5 cm. This spirit was carved by a shaman to help a person suffering lung ailment to combat the evil spirits who caused it.

Tlingit shaman with dagger and typically long shaman's hair style, from the late 1800s. National

Museum of Natural History, Smithsonian Institution, E073837. 24 cm.

Nanai guardian of fishing, Kalgama, collected in 1913 by I.A. Lopatin on the Amur River. Vladivostok Maritime Museum, Russia, #917-96. 24.5 cm. A Nanai fisherman offers his first catch to Kalgama, smearing the fish's blood on the figure's mouth. A shaman will carve Kalgama's companion, Dadgifu, in the event of unsuccessful fishing (see Fig. 72).

76

76.

Shaman's drum cover with helping spirits

Udegei shaman's drum cover from Khor River, Russia, collected by N.A. Zorin in 1907. Vladivostok Maritime Museum, Russia, #2180-8a. 74 cm.

This drum cover is made of birch bark, cotton, and leather. Various animal spirits are painted on the bark, including bears, dragon-like creatures, snakes, tigers, and birds, as well as two suns often found on the drum itself and on shamans' coats in many Siberian cultures.

Shamans are healers (chasing away evil spirits that cause sickness), priests (honoring ancestors and conducting ceremonies), and ambassadors (negotiating with the Masters of the Animals and other spirits). They travel to the land above and the land below with the help of their drum, belts, rattles, helping spirits, and occasionally hallucinogenics. Shamans divine the future, identify spirits, and insure that the community follows rules and taboos.

77.

Home guardian

Chukchi hanging amulet, guardian of family prosperity, from Anadyr, Chukotka, Russia, collected in 1892 by L.F. Grinevetskii. The dark pigment is soot from its stay in the house, and it bears traces of food around the mouth, having been fed by its hosts. It was hung by a baleen link. Vladivostok Maritime Museum, Russia, #943-7. 16.5 cm.

77

78.

Shaman's belt with bells

Udegei shaman's belt used during shamanistic performance, collected by Yu. M. Degtiarev in the village of Gvasiugi on the Amur River, Siberia. Vladivostok Maritime Museum, Russia, #4018-6. 30 cm.

The belt is made of leather, metal, and grass. The bells, in concert with the drum-beating during the dance, attract the spirits and allow them to meet with the shaman for a dialogue, a fight, or difficult negotiations.

78

79.

Night and day mask

Athapaskan (Ingalik) black and white female mask with labret and nose pendant, collected by Edward W. Nelson on the Kuskokwim River, Alaska, in 1879. National Museum of Natural History, Smithsonian Institution, #E064242. 47 cm.

79

80.

Gang of spirits

Nanai (?) gang of spirits from the Amur River region, collected by Stanislaw Poniatowski in 1919. National Museum of Natural History, Smithsonian Institution, #E303728. 7 to 12 cm.

80

81

82

81.

Shaman and helping spirit

Udegei shaman-ancestor figure riding his helping spirit, collected in 1959 by V.G. Lar'kin in the village of Gvasiugi. Vladivostok Maritime Museum, Russia, #4511-19. 35.5 cm (beast) and 27 cm (shaman).

The wooden shaman is dressed in leather and fur. It is a powerful protector for the practicing shaman, as it represents a shaman traveling to the world of spirits on the back of his helping spirit, a tiger-like beast.

82.

Ceremonial garments

Nanai shaman's bib collected in 1905 by B.O. Pilsudsky in the village of Troitskoe, and Oroch ceremonial belt ummu *with pouch* sekty *collected in 1945 by M.P. Biriustiukova in the village of Us'na-Orochnaia. Vladivostok Maritime Museum, Russia, #893-240 (bib), and #1016-6 and-7 (belt). 39 cm and 182 cm.*

Some of the creatures on the bib are similar to those on the Udegei drum cover (Fig. 76). They are oriented towards to head of the shaman wearing the bib, in order to help him, rather than painted for the benefit of the audience. The sekty *pouch contains grass (tobacco?) and is made of various furs.*

Food is a community event in both Siberia and Alaska. Hunting is traditionally reserved for men, while women fish, pick berries, and gather plants.

Cuisine: Food for People, Food for Spirits

For this work the women weave beautiful baskets; the men help by carving ingenious small combs to prepare the grass for twining and coiling into baskets.

Food also has a spiritual dimension. Both Alaskan and Siberian peoples traditionally share food with spirits, Ancestors, or Masters, serving it in special dishes.

Artifacts rank from delicate and ornate to massive, simple, and rustic, but always display a keen sense of design. In nomadic cultures where little is carried, dishes, spoons, knives, and cups are pretty to the eye, comfortable to the hand, and pleasant to the mouth.

83

83.

Basketry for berries and beauty

From top, right to left:

Athapaskan basket collected by I. Applegate in Interior Alaska in the 1880s, made of birch bark, red glass beads with white hearts, and leather. National Museum of Natural History, Smithsonian Institution, #E277596. 17.8 cm.

Tlingit berry basket with "shaman's hat design", from about 1910, made of split spruce root, grass, and fern frond. University of Alaska Museum, Fairbanks, #UA840-31. 10.5 cm.

Nivkh wooden spoon from northern Sakhalin Island, late 1800s-early 1900s. Sakhalin Regional Museum, Russia, #947-11. 25 cm. Small Aleut basket made by Christine Dushkin from Sandpoint, Alaska, in 1980-81,

with wined grass and thread embroidery. University of Alaska Museum, Fairbanks, #UA81-3-182AB. 7 cm.

Yupik grass comb from the Kuskokwim region, Alaska, made in the early 1900s of bone with hinged bone blade. This ingenious and delightful small comb was collected by G.B. Gordon. National Museum of the American Indian, Smithsonian Institution, #1/6658. 7 cm.

Prehistoric Eskimo old ivory grass comb with engraved circle from St. Lawrence Island, Alaska, collected by Henry B. Collins in 1931. National Museum of Natural History, Smithsonian Institution, #A353766. 4.7 cm.

Tsimshian cedar bark basket made by Violet Booth from Metlakatla, Alaska, in 1980. University of Alaska Museum, Fairbanks, #UA81-3-44. 10 cm.

84.

Evenk scoop

Evenk birch bark scoop from the Amur River, Siberia, 1989. Khabarovsk Regional Museum, #9736-1. 14.6 cm.

84

85.

Closed baskets and box
From left to right:

Koryak basket from the Ghizhiginsk area, collected by F.K. Gek in 1885. Vladivostok Maritime Museum, Russia, #913-94. 19 cm.

Yupik grass basket made by Betsy Altsuk from Nightmute, Alaska, in 1981. University of

Alaska Museum, Fairbanks, #UA81-3-160AB. 14 cm.

Ulchi box to carry dishes during reindeer herding trips, from the late 1800s-early 1900s, made of wood and reindeer skin, with glass trade beads. Sakhalin Regional Museum, Russia, #990-2. 26.5 cm.

85

86.

Black and white spoons and baskets
Nanai (round) and Oroch (square) birch baskets from the Khabarovsk region, Siberia. The round basket was made by Nanai artist A.K. Samar in 1991. Khabarovsk Regional Museum, Russia, #VX-312 and #490. 13.5 cm and 20 cm.

Koniag bone spoon collected in 1935 by Ales Hrdlicka on Kodiak Island, Alaska, dated around A.D. 1400, and Tlingit engraved mountain goat horn spoon from the late 1800s. National Museum of Natural History, Smithsonian Institution, #A377796 and #E176708. 14.6 cm and 17.5 cm.

87.

Simple and hearty beauty

Yupik wooden spoons from the lower Kuskokwim region, from the 1920s (wide), and from southwest Alaska, from the 1800s (small) University of Alaska Museum, Fairbanks,#UA610-5916 and #UA64-64-104. 21 cm and 15.2 cm.

"Crowbill's Drinking Cup," inscribed Chukchi container from Plover Bay, Chukotka, Siberia, made in the late1800s-early 1900s, of wood and horn. National Museum of Natural History, Smithsonian Institution, #E292261. 17 cm.

88.

Ainu food ritual

Ainu wooden plate and ikupasuy *(ritual libation sticks), from southern Sakhalin Island, late 1800s-early 1900s. Sakhalin Regional Museum, Russia, #87-16 (plate) and 48-12, 14, 17, and 19. 19.5 cm (plate), and 30.5 to 35.5 cm (sticks).*

Besides holding their long mustaches out of the sake drunk in honor of their ancestors, the ikupasuy *are considered the mediators between humans and gods, speaking to them in a symbolic language encoded in the art.*

88

89

89.

Yupik small bowl

*Yupik red and black painted bowl
with fish or shrimp design,
collected by Henry B. Collins on
Nunivak Island, Alaska, in 1927.
National Museum of Natural
History, Smithsonian Institution,
#A340180. 12.4 cm*

90

90.

Ulu

Alaska Inupiaq ulu from the late 1800s to early 1900s, made of wood, steel, and nails. University of Alaska Museum, Fairbanks, #UA91-9-8. 15 cm.

91.

Nivkh bear festival

Nivkh wooden bear festival scoop and spoon with bear figures from northern Sakhalin Island, late 1800s-early 1900s. Sakhalin Regional Museum, Russia, #944-2 and #948. 61.8 cm and 23.5 cm.

The figure of the bear is central to the Ainu, Nivkh, and groups from the Amur River, as the Ancestor and God who descended to visit humans in a bear shape. During the bear festival, villagers sacrificed a captured cub raised by a woman from the community as her own child. They dressed it in ceremonial costume and offered it food at a banquet so that it would take back to the realm of gods a benevolent message from the village. These two artifacts were used ritually in this festival and carry images of the bear. The festival, abandoned after 1950, is being revived.

91

The peoples of the Alaskan and Siberian interior depend on a close relationship with land and animals for survival. Animals provide the hunter and trapper with meat, the seamstress with fur and skins, and the trader with items for trade with coastal peoples.

People, Animals, and the Land

Hunting is the chief means of living off the land, and specialized equipment—from snow goggles to snowshoes—was invented for arctic hunting.

In Northeastern Siberia reindeer herding has roots deep in the past. The distinction between interior and coastal peoples there is mainly between sea mammal hunters and reindeer breeders, rather than sea hunters and land hunters. Reindeer herding was never a traditional Alaskan economic activity.

92.

Udegei hunting panache

Udegei hunter's hat called bogdo *made by Irina Ivanovna Kialungzioga, from the village of Gvasiugi, Amur River, Siberia, in 1984-86. The materials she used are fabric, various furs, including squirrel for the tuft, silk, and leather. Khabarovsk Regional Museum, Russia, #9123-3 (hat). 27 cm.*

Alaska hunting and trapping

Prehistoric Eskimo child's ice creeper collected on Seward Peninsula, Alaska, by Karl Lomen in 1926, made of ivory. National Museum of Natural History, Smithsonian Institution, #A332255. 4.7 cm. Ice creepers were secured to the boot with leather thongs to avoid sliding.

Western Eskimo wooden snow goggles collected in Norton Sound, Alaska, by Lucien Turner in the 1870s. National Museum of Natural History, Smithsonian Institution, #E 024340. 13.2 cm.

Inupiaq snow goggles made by Elijah Kikinyah, from Anaktuvuk Pass, Alaska, in 1969, with wood, caribou leather, and graphite. University of Alaska Museum, Fairbanks, #UA69-58-17C. 14 cm.

The narrow slits allow the hunter to see, while protecting the eyes against the harsh reflection of light on the snow and ice.

Inupiaq snares, on the right from Teller, Alaska, 1950s, made of wood, baleen, and bird bone; on the left, made by Simon Paneak from Anaktuvuk Pass, Alaska, in 1969, of a willow twig and braided sinew. University

of Alaska Museum, Fairbanks, #UA593 and #UA69-68-4. 20 cm and 46 cm.

Prehistoric ivory Eskimo projectile point from Northern Alaska, and grey chert projectile point from the Denbigh culture, Alaska, about 1500 B.C.. University of Alaska Museum, Fairbanks, #UA81-86-463 and #CS-66-690. 4.6 cm and 4 cm.

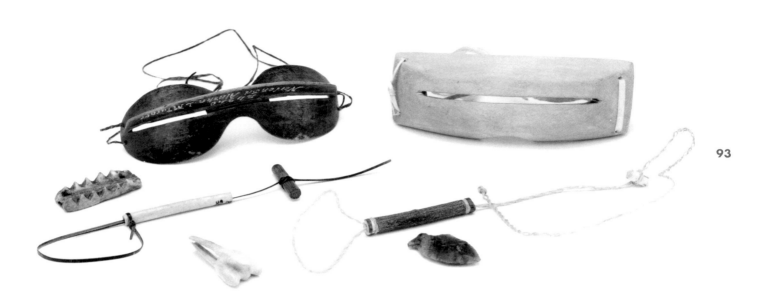

93

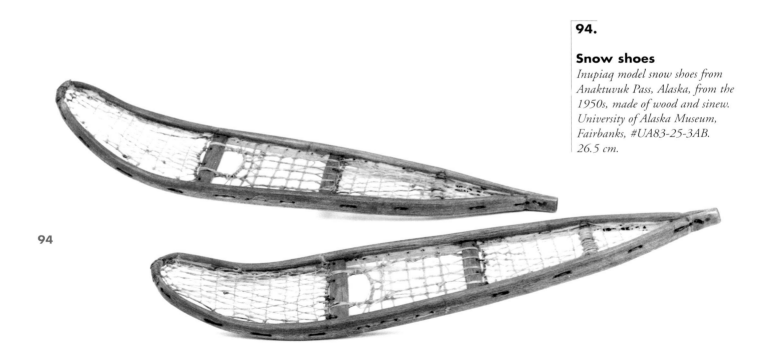

94

Snow shoes

Inupiaq model snow shoes from Anaktuvuk Pass, Alaska, from the 1950s, made of wood and sinew. University of Alaska Museum, Fairbanks, #UA83-25-3AB. 26.5 cm.

95.

Kerek dog spirits

Kerek dog spirits from Northern Kamchatka, Siberia, collected in 1855 by F.K. Gek. Vladivostok Maritime Museum, Russia, #1132-7, -8, and -11. 5 to 7 cm. Very few artifacts from the Kerek culture are found in museum collections. A very small number of Kerek people (around 400) live on the coast between the Chukchi and the Koryak areas. The markings on these dogs, especially the one in the center, too numerous and complex to be mere representations of harness, attest to the importance of dogs and their domestication in this culture, as in the two neighboring cultures.

96.

Sleds

Athapaskan sled model with dogs and driver, made by Micah Malcom from Eagle, Alaska, in 1988, with birch and pine. University of Alaska Museum, Fairbanks, #UA88-3-6. 42 cm. Model of an Ulchi sled called buchi, *from the village of Bulava, Amur River, 1990. Khabarovsk Regional Museum, Russia #9742-26. 16.5 cm.*

96

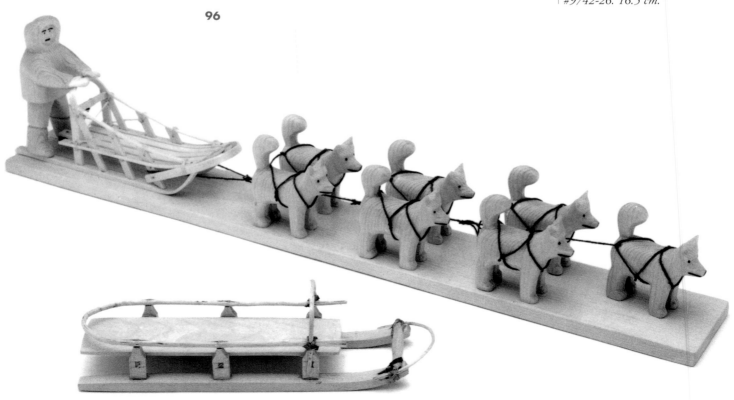

97.

Sleds

Bottom: Eskimo sled model from Norton Sound, Alaska, collected in 1910 by Henry B. Collins. The runners are made of ivory, the body of wood, red pigment, and sinew. National Museum of Natural History, Smithsonian Institution, #E260534.

Top: Koryak sled model from Ghizhiga, Siberia, collected in 1886 by G.G. Poliakov, made of wood and leather. Vladivostok Maritime Museum, Russia, #912-20. 36 cm. A full-sized sled might measure 2 to 2.5 meters in length, and be pulled by 10 to 12 dogs.

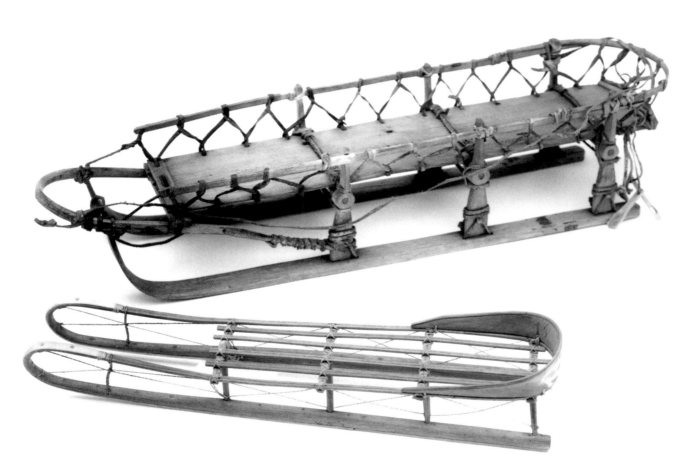

97

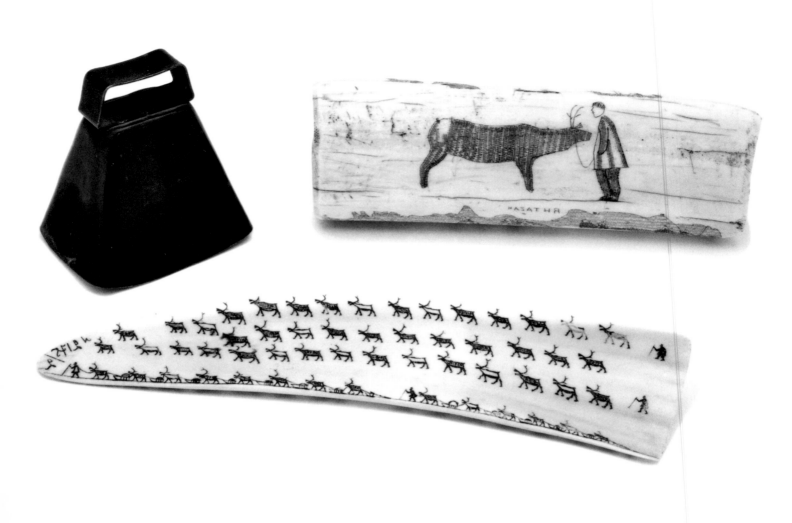

98.

Reindeer herding

Alaska commercially made steel reindeer bell from the 1900s, collected by Otto Geist. University of Alaska Museum, Fairbanks, #UA64-21-160. 9 cm.

Top: Chunk of Chukchi or Siberian Eskimo walrus tusk collected in 1948 (see also Fig. 37 p. 49). Vladivostok Maritime Museum, Russia, #2688. 16 cm.

Chukchi walrus tusk with scene of reindeer herding and sledges from Ghizhiga Bay, Siberia, collected in 1922 by V.K. Arsen'ev. Vladivostok Maritime Museum, Russia, #1211-1. 23.5 cm.

Siberians have herded reindeer for more than 2,000 years; the Chukchi and Koryak adopted large-scale herding in the late 1600s. Reindeer herding was introduced into Alaska in the 1890s, but it was never a success; the idea of holding animals "captive" offended the beliefs of traditional hunting peoples.

99.

Hunting paraphernalia
Udegei uma *(hunter's belt),*
konikhi *(knife sheath), and* ladu
*(pouch), made by Irina Ivanovna
Kialungzioga, from the village
of Gvasiugi, Amur River, Siberia,
in 1984-86. Fabric, fur, silk,
and leather. Khabarovsk Regional
Museum, Russia #8695-20.
42 cm (belt).*

*Udegei hunter's mitt from the
1950s. Khabarovsk Regional
Museum, Russia #5808. 30 cm.
The thumb has an opening at
the base, protected by the flap, to
allow the hunter to operate his
weapon without taking the mitt
off. It is as lavishly and brightly
decorated as the rest of the
hunter's outfit.*

99

For peoples of the North Pacific coasts, the sea is the center of their economic and spiritual lives.

People, Animals, and the Sea

The sea is rich with fish and mammals for the fisherman and hunter; it tempers the climate; and it offers a means of transportation, for which many types of boats were devised. All of these circumstances have made coastal cultures distinctly different from those of the interior. The beauty and sophistication of sea-hunting equipment reflect the sea's central importance.

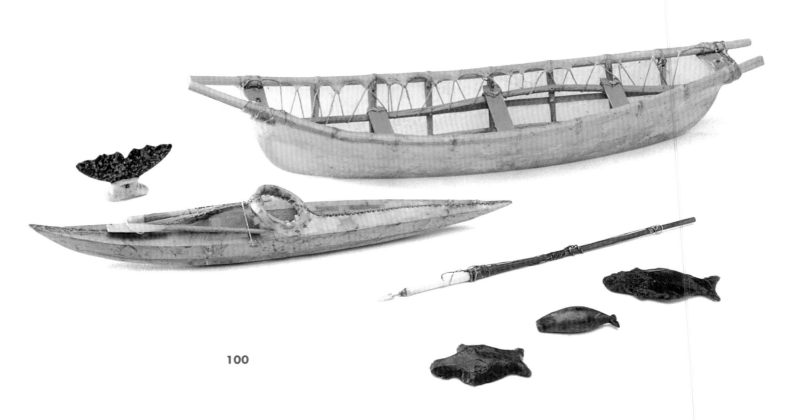

100

100.

Hunting the whale

Whale hunting involved magic as well as skill; hunters carried amulets for a successful hunt. Aleut and Eskimo hunters wore special costumes and magnificent bentwood visors to honor the spirits of the animals they hunted. The Koryak held elaborate ceremonies to greet the captured whale as a high-ranking guest. Smaller sea mammals and fish were also honored with respectful rituals and with ornate weapons and lures.

Inupiaq umiak (baidara) model made by Victor Swan from Kivalina, Alaska, in 1970, of wood, scraped caribou hide, and cordage. University of Alaska Museum, Fairbanks, #UA70-50-185. 31.7 cm.

Inupiaq kayak model from the Bering Strait, Alaska, from the early 1960s, made of gutskin, wood, and ivory. University of Alaska Museum, Fairbanks, #UA67-132-6. 24.3 cm.

Inupiaq stone and ivory labret (lip plug) in the shape of a whale tail, collected in the1870s by Edward W. Nelson on King Island, Alaska. National Museum of Natural History, Smithsonian Institution, #E043757. 5.1 cm.

Aleut harpoon model from the Commander Islands, Russia, collected in 1899 by N.M. Tilman, made of wood, ivory, thread, and red pigments. Vladivostok Maritime Museum, Russia, #2160-7. 18 cm.

Three Inupiaq whaling charms from the 1700s, collected by Henry B. Collins in 1929 in Point Hope, Alaska, from the collections of the National Museum of Natural History, Smithsonian Institution, left to right: red chert whale-man charm #A344673, 5 cm; ivory whale charm pierced at the blow-hole #A347714, 4 cm; black chert whale charm #A347715, 5.9 cm.

101.

Sea hunting visor
Yupik hunter's wooden visor from Rasboinsky, Yukon River, Alaska, painted black, blue, and green, collected in the 1870s by Edward W. Nelson. National Museum of Natural History, Smithsonian Institution, #E049068. 16 cm.

101

102.

Fishing and sea hunting gear
From left to right:

Prehistoric Eskimo old ivory sinker from St. Lawrence Island, Alaska, collected by Moreau Chambers in 1933. National Museum of Natural History, Smithsonian Institution, #A370735. 10.8 cm.

Inupiaq fish hook made by Mark Cleveland from Ambler, Alaska, before 1970, of aluminum, nail, plastic, baleen, steel, copper wire, and thread. University of Alaska Museum, Fairbanks, #UA70-50-65. 18 cm.

Inupiaq fishing lure from the Diomede Islands, collected by Edward W. Nelson in the 1870s, made of stone, bone, sinew, glass beads, puffin beaks, and an iron

hook. National Museum of Natural History, Smithsonian Institution, #E063631. 9 cm.

Prehistoric Aleut ivory float plug from Amaknak Island, Alaska. University of Alaska Museum, Fairbanks, #UA68-62-32. 2.7 cm.

Athapaskan wooden shuttle for weaving nets from Rampart, Alaska, 20th century. University of Alaska Museum, Fairbanks, #957. 18 cm.

Prehistoric Aleut bone projectile point from Amaknak Island, Alaska. University of Alaska Museum, Fairbanks, #UA68-62-254. 13 cm.

Prehistoric Eskimo ivory harpoon head collected by Henry B. Collins on Punuk Island, Alaska, in

1929. National Museum of Natural History, Smithsonian Institution, #A343173. 9 cm.

Prehistoric Aleut ivory fish hook and harpoon head from Amaknak Island, Alaska. University of Alaska Museum, Fairbanks, #UA68-62-99 and UA68-62-124. Both 5.5 cm.

Koniag miniature whaling harpoon from Kodiak Island, Alaska, A.D. 1400, made of ivory and slate, collected by Ales Hrdlicka in 1937. National Museum of Natural History, Smithsonian Institution, #A 390553. 5 cm.

Inupiaq ivory net gauge from Point Barrow, Alaska, dated from the late 1800s. University of Alaska Museum, Fairbanks #UA81-86-189. 11 cm.

Prehistoric wooden stylized figure of an Eskimo hunter wearing a bentwood hat, from St. Lawrence Island, Alaska, collected by Moreau Chambers in 1933. National Museum of Natural History, Smithsonian Institution, #A369829. 4 cm.

Inupiaq metal seal harpoon from Point Hope, Alaska, 20th century, collected by Henry B. Collins in 1929. National Museum of Natural History, Smithsonian Institution, #A347819. 5.4 cm.

Three prehistoric Eskimo ivory prongs for fish or bird spear from St. Lawrence Island, Alaska. University of Alaska Museum, Fairbanks #2-1934-2243, #2-1934-2266 and #2-1934-2302. 5 cm.

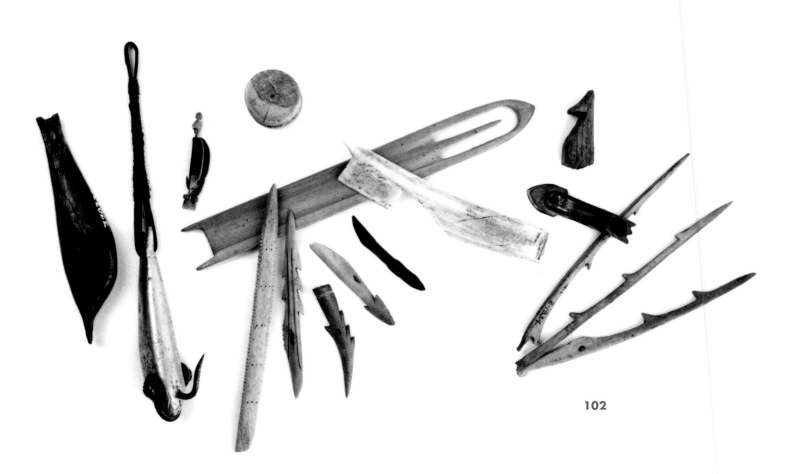

102

103.

Tlingit canoe

Tlingit wooden canoe model from Yakutat, Alaska, from the 1800s. National Museum of the American Indian, Smithsonian Institution, #16/8476. 29.9 cm.

Until airplanes were used, seas and rivers offered the most effective means of transportation; the first migrants to Alaska from Asia might indeed have come by boat (see pp. 37 and 42-43).

103

104

104.

Ulchi boats

Ulchi boat models from the village of Bulava, Amur River, 1990. Khabarovsk Regional Museum, Russia #9742-24 and #9742-25. 27 cm and 16.5 cm.

105

105.

Aleut kayak

Aleut model of a two-man baidarka (or kayak) from the Commander Islands, Russia, collected in 1891 by N.M. Tilman. Made of wood, gutskin, bone, fabric, and glass beads. Vladivostok Maritime Museum, Russia, #2305. 49 cm.

Floats for an actual kayak are made of inflated sealskins, and attached to the harpoon in order to slow down the wounded game, and allow the hunter to locate and retrieve it later when the animal sinks. The Aleut are very skilled at maneuvering kayaks, which can also be made as three-man crafts. Aleut hunters would not hesitate to hunt a large whale, armed with magic protection from ancestor-whalers and with aconite poison smeared on their harpoon.

106.

Floating face

Asian Eskimo float plug from Big Diomede Island, Russia, collected in 1885 by F.K. Gek, made of wood and blue glass beads for the eyes. Vladivostok Maritime Museum, Russia, #1132-34. 7 cm.

This delightfully carved plug is used to close the opening of an inflated sealskin float, and carries the friendly face of a person with a frowning mouth, symbolic of both females and sea mammals.

106

107

107.

Whale effigy to take along

Inupiaq wooden whale effigy from Little Diomede Island, Alaska, from the 1800s, collected by Henry B. Collins in 1929. National Museum of Natural History, Smithsonian Institution, #347918. 20 cm.

Ritually potent quartz crystals were inserted into the blow-hole and the eyes, and there is a space under the board in the center where a large crystal was kept. The board was lashed on the umiak through the holes on the sides, for good luck when hunting.

Each cultural group in Alaska and Siberia looked upon all others as "strangers."

Warfare and trade were the main types of contact between neighboring native groups—and between continents— and existed for centuries before outsiders arrived from beyond the North Pacific Rim.

Very ancient Chinese influence can be seen in clothing and artifacts from Siberia's Amur River region. Drawn by the fur trade, Russia expanded into northeastern Siberia in the 1600s and into Alaska in the 1700s. American whaling ships arrived in the 1850s. Each had its influence on the cultures living there.

108

Trade

Ancient Native trading networks across Bering Strait expanded by the late 1700s, when new products became available. Tobacco, beads, and metal were among the most popular trade items. Clockwise from the top:

Yupik snuff box with a face, collected by Edward W. Nelson in Kushunuk, Alaska, in the 1870s. The eyes and labrets are made of ivory. National Museum of Natural History, Smithsonian Institution, #E036260. 7.8 cm.

Alaska peg calendar collected in the 1950s by Rhoda Thomas, University of Alaska Museum, Fairbanks, #UA67-98-278AB. 22.5 cm. Missionaries gave such calendars to Native converts to help them keep track of weekdays and remember when to go to church.

Athapaskan doll mittens from Rampart, Alaska, made between 1908 and 1920, of smoked hide, plucked beaver fur, and glass beads. University of Alaska Museum, Fairbanks, #UA900-79AB. 11 cm. The American eagle is beaded on the back of the mitts.

Eskimo pipe from Norton Sound, Alaska, from the 1870s, collected by Edward W. Nelson. Made of wood, iron, leather, brass, and beads. National Museum of Natural History, Smithsonian Institution, #E032870. 19 cm. A metal piece for cleaning the pipe bowl is attached to the pipe with beadwork strands.

Ainu bronze pipe bowl from Southern Sakhalin Island, late 1800s-early 1900s. Sakhalin Regional Museum, Russia, #VX B/N. 7.8 cm.

Tlingit wooden pipe bowl from Chatham Strait, Alaska, from the 1880s. National Museum of the American Indian, Smithsonian Institution, #9246. 6 cm. The bowl opens like the mouth of a bird-like creature.

Yupik snuff box in the shape of a fish, collected by Edward W. Nelson in Kulwoguwigumut, Kuskokwim Bay, Alaska, in the 1870s. National Museum of Natural History, Smithsonian Institution, #E036282. 9 cm. The lid is underneath the belly of the fish.

Aleut basket bottle made by Mary Hillhouse from Nikolski, Alaska, in 1982, of twined grass and thread embroidery over a glass bottle with metal lid. University of Alaska Museum, Fairbanks, #83-3-30-ab. 11.2 cm. The fine basket-making tradition of the Aleuts weaves itself around a Euro-American bottle.

Trade glass beads collected in St. Lawrence Island, Alaska, in the late 1800s-early 1900s. University of Alaska Museum, Fairbanks, #UA71-34-1. 35 cm.

In the center: Ainu woman's blue glass beads from Sakhalin Island, Russia, from the late 1800s-early 1900s. Sakhalin Regional Museum, Russia, #58. 70 cm.

Tobacco box and pipe

Koryak snuff box from Kamchatka, Siberia, about 1950, made of mountain goat horn, wood, and a metal chain and metal pipe cleaner. Kamchatka Regional Museum, Russia, #8-E-180. 8 cm.

Tlingit stone pipe bowl from Yakutat, Alaska, with three human faces, from the 1880s. National Museum of the American Indian, Smithsonian Institution, #9285. 2.8 cm.

109

110, 111, 112, 113.

Scenes of warfare

Asian Eskimo engraved walrus tusk with scenes of battles, made by Yukau from Uelen, Chukotka, Russia, in 1947. Vladivostok Maritime Museum, Russia, #1206-1. Tusk: 55 cm.

The event represented is the unsuccessful attempt by Russian Major Plavlutskii to conquer the Chukchi in the 18th century, with the help of the Yakut. One side represents the Yakut warriors leaving the wooded areas with reindeer and Yakut sleds, and carrying a flag with a Russian icon. The other side depicts the battle itself in a Chukchi village on the tundra .

114.

Geared for warfare

Prehistoric Eskimo bone wrist guard for bowman from Point Hope, Alaska, and two prehistoric Eskimo bone plates from an armor suit from St. Lawrence Island, Alaska, collected by Henry B. Collins in 1929. National Museum of Natural History, Smithsonian Institution, #A347829 and #A355982. 7.8 cm and 14 cm.

Prehistoric Eskimo old ivory war arrow point from Western Alaska. National Museum of Natural History, Smithsonian Institution, #A333291. 16.5 cm.

Chukchi or Asian Eskimo walrus ivory warrior figure in armor and shield from Chukotka, Russia, collected in 1885 by F.K. Gek. Vladivostok Maritime Museum, Russia, #1132-18. 3 cm.

114

115.

Spear point

Nivkh copper spear point from Sakhalin Island, Russia, from the late 1800s-early 1900s. Sakhalin Regional Museum, Russia, #1668-278. 56.2 cm.

115

Alaska Native Graphic Arts

Susan W. Fair

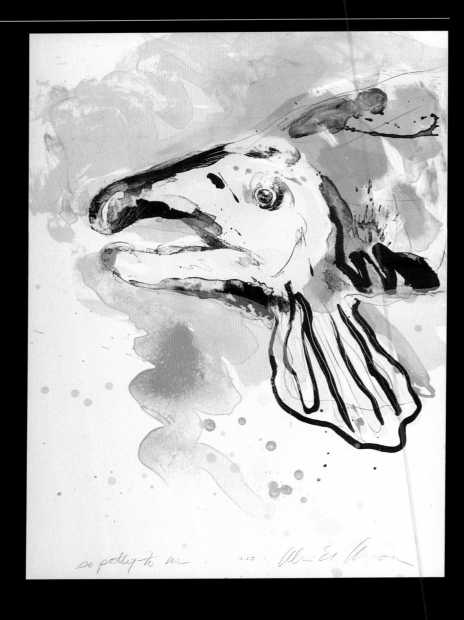

116.

*"So Pretty to Me,"
1960, by Alvin
Amason, Aleut artist,
Fairbanks, Alaska
(b. 1948, Kodiak).
Collection of the
artist. 76x56 cm.*

Graphic arts, the embellishment of flat surfaces with decorative or symbolic designs or pictorial representation, is a well-developed form of expression among all Alaska Native groups. In the north, Eskimo graphic traditions are indigenous, dating from prehistoric zig-zag incising and simple border designs, which evolved into figures, and then into complex pictographic scenes (Ard 1970:51, 55; 1982:275; Giddings 1967:194).

In southeast Alaska, a highly complex graphics tradition flourished among Northwest Coast peoples, celebrating myths, history, house groups, and clans through crest designs on wood, skin, and textiles. In the 1700s or earlier, when Russian fur traders or Siberian Native entrepreneurs introduced glass beads to Alaska Natives, elaborate floral

beadwork on cloth and skin began to dominate Athapaskan graphic arts. In the 19th century the Aleut ornamented wooden hats and visors with polychrome paintings of birds and animals, scenes of domestic life and hunting exploits, and mythical figures, as well as elaborate geometric borders and motifs (Fitzhugh and Crowell 1988:164-65). In interior Alaska, George Thornton Emmons, collecting among Athapaskans in the early 1900s, obtained simple rectangular bone stretchers engraved with geometric designs made by the Tahltan for their packstraps; carefully balanced and textured, they imitate porcupine quillwork, as do incised designs on some early birchbark baskets (Emmons 1911, fig. 12).

In the past, simple graphics (e.g. circle and dot designs) might convey complex meaning, while some of the most complex designs (e.g. the swirls and curves that ornament Old Bering Sea implements (Fig. 18) may be primarily decorative. Simple graphic designs were also applied as marks of ownership on personal property or as references to totemic animals that protected their owners (Himmelheber 1987 [1938]: 24-25). On Kodiak Island and in northwest Alaska, such proprietary designs were also used in prehistoric times. Among the Chukchi, Bogoras noted that the eyes of killed bears and whales were pierced, "and the viscous fluid from them, mixed with soot, [was] used for painting the paddles of the boat in a special manner" to commemorate a successful hunt (1904-09 15:408).

Circles, Dots, Spirals, and Raven's Footprints

Circular motifs have been used among nearly all Native American groups from prehistory to the present. Incised and painted spirals, dots, dotted circles, ovoids, and rosettes represent the eye while addressing cosmic concepts such as physical and transcendental functions of sight, peripherality, spiritual wholeness, and transformation—what Ann Fienup Riordan has called "the eye of awareness" (1987:43-47; Smith and Spier 1927; Fitzhugh and Kaplan 1982:202).

Eye motifs or ovoids, which are used extensively in stylized Northwest Coast graphics, often signify joints or points of connection (Holm 1965:37), as do dots or circles in other groups (Fienup-Riordan 1987, Schuster 1951, Bogoras 1904-09). Yupik and Inupiaq Eskimos once decorated almost every type of implement with nucleated circles, from women's needle cases and bag handles to the drill bows collected by Kotzebue during his first contact with the Inupiaq of Kotzebue Sound in 1816, and on engravings decorating 2,000-year-old Okvik dolls and weapons (Figs. 18, 31).

In Aleut art, circles and dots are often incised on carved and painted spirals (volutes), which may simultaneously represent a bird's beak and a phallus, referring, as Lydia Black suggests, to earthly abundance as well as a universal system of "cosmological reproduction" (Black 1991:43). When attached to the sides of a hunting hat or painted on its surface, the circle and volute also resemble wings, linking the hunter with such powerful birds as the thunderbird and eagle, and with magical flight (Black 1991:38).

The track of Raven is another common motif among Alaska Native peoples. Simply wrought, Raven's footprint is composed of three or four straight lines, although the track may sometimes be incorporated into more complex borders and designs (Fitzhugh and Crowell 1988:305). These simple lines are a graphic reminder of the beginnings of cultural time, for among most Alaska Native peoples, Raven is regarded as creator. Other simple linear motifs include skeletal patterns and "lifelines." When used to illustrate skeletal patterns, spurred straight-line combinations are often connected to concentric circles, thus linking the "interior" or biologic features of the animal portrayed with external physical and cosmic realms (Fitzhugh and Kaplan 1982:198-201).

117.

"Kayak" by Sylvester Ayek, Inupiaq artist, Anchorage and Nome, Alaska (b. 1940, King Island). Anchorage Museum of History and Art, #73-097-5.

118.

"In Homage," 1974, by John Kailukiak, Yupik artist, Tooksook Bay, Alaska (b. 1951, Tooksook Bay). Anchorage Museum of History and Art, #75-040-1.

119.

"Engraving and Etching," 1976, by Lawrence Ahvakana, Inupiaq artist, Suquamish, Washington (b. 1946, Barrow). Private collection.

117

118

119

Early Graphics

The earliest known form of graphic art is work on stone in the form of pictographs and petroglyphs in natural settings: rock outcroppings, caves, and prominent boulders. In the north, these works are rare, usually executed in remote locations rather than permanent settlements. They are probably the work of men—hunters on the move some distance from home. In southeast Alaska, petroglyphs are often found near ancient village sites (Emmons/de Laguna 1991:78). Graphics on stone in that region may have recorded the movements of particular clans and groups into new territories, celebrated important tribal events, or marked specific communal interests such as plentiful salmon streams (ibid.). Detailed incising has also been found on pebbles at prehistoric sites in far-flung regions, including Yakutat (de Laguna 1964:169), Point Hope, Cape Krusenstern, late prehistoric sites at Kodiak (Fitzhugh and Crowell 1988:134), and other areas (Ard 1970:108-10).

A less durable though highly visible form of graphic art was the tattooing and painting of the human body. This art is known primarily through the descriptions of non-Native explorers, the sketchbooks of artists who accompanied them, and later accounts of mariners, teachers, and anthropologists, and from the work of at least one Native graphic artist, St. Lawrence Island Yupik Florence Nupok (1908-71), who was very interested in body decoration and frequently illustrated tattoos. Today, among the Siberian Yupik, Alaska Yupik and Inupiaq, some female elders have tattoos on their hands and faces, and some less visible tattooing may still be done among St. Lawrence Island Eskimos, both men and women, to indicate affiliation with specific kin groups and to celebrate certain events. In some regions, young women were tattooed at puberty. The marks on their chins were said to be "sewn" on, emphasizing connections between domestic skills and standards of female beauty (Chaussonnet 1988:224; Moore and Johnson 1986:108).

In another form of personal adornment among Alaska Natives prior to European contact, the body was pierced for nose ornaments and labrets (lip plugs) (Fig. 61). Labrets carved from stone, wood, or ivory were often worn in pairs, below the mouth on both sides. Labrets were common among northern Eskimos who wore pieced skin parkas that had gores of lighter skins on each side of the chest. The graphic symmetry of the labrets and the tusk-shaped gores linked the wearer metaphorically with the natural world by emulating an important animal—the walrus (see Fitzhugh and Kaplan 1982:169; Chaussonnet and Driscoll 1994:111).

Today, northern skin-sewers still make fancy squirrel-skin parkas with miniature blocks of squirrel-skin piecing at the back of the hood, as well as other graphic elements. Though the specific meanings of these "fancy" skin graphics are unknown, they have magical implications. Through such designs, the adorned human body becomes a graphic text, transmitting messages about ethnicity, home village, hunting prowess, sewing skills, and other topics (Schevill 1986:1-5).

120.

"This My Mother Mary, and Baby George," 1958, by George Ahgupuk, Inupiaq artist, Anchorage. Pen and Ink on Caribou Skin. Alaska State Museum, Juneau, #V-A-725.

Gender and Graphics Production

Among Native peoples, men generally work with rigid materials, while women's work more often involves pliant raw materials such as skins and grasses. Even today, materials are divided along male and female lines, although this is changing somewhat as traditional roles are modified and as new materials become available. Women have also had a somewhat more restricted access to certain materials, as well as less familiarity with the tools for working them and, possibly, the type of subject matter used historically in decoration.

Ivory, for example, which is obtained by hunting walrus, and whalebone, which is found when traveling and beachcombing, are usually collected by men who travel together in hunting crews and fraternal groups. Ivory is processed almost exclusively by men and often inscribed with pictorial representations. Men's connection with the sea is underscored throughout the process. In addition, hunting and trade exposed men to new people and fresh ideas that women were less likely to experience firsthand.

Women also gather materials in groups, but almost always on land. The symbols used by women, sewn into fancy parkas or woven into baskets, tend to be non-representational and are usually worked into an object rather than applied to it (with the exception of felt and skin appliqué, which has been popular among north Alaska Eskimo women for some time [Ray 1969:38-41]). Gender-based divisions of materials, tools, and symbols may have some connection to the transfer of ideas and symbols to paper, for it appears that—unlike Canadian Inuit women—few women work in that medium in Alaska.

In southeast Alaska, the graphic arts of men were most often produced on wood as pattern boards, house screens, house posts, and other objects. These works of art were often monumental (and grew even larger when metal tools became available), requiring the felling of large trees, from which planks were hewn, then carved or painted. This was not considered women's work, and only now are women beginning to break into totemic carving and painting crest designs on wood.

Today, serigraphy (silkscreen printing) is an established industry on the Northwest Coast, particularly in Canada. This art is produced mainly by men (Hall, Blackman, and Rickard 1981:49-54); the graphics made by women from these regions are generally worked into soft goods—baskets, blankets, robes, and other traditional garments. Men intervene in the production of some soft goods, such as Chilkat robes, which require a pattern board created by men, and woven spruce root hats, which men paint with crest designs.

Graphic designs in basketry were an important means of female expression. Some patterns, like "Mouth Track of the Wood-worm" and Tongue of the Thunderbird," are thought to refer to myths recalling clan origins and history (Paul 1944:47,49), but most are simple, lyrical, and representational, such as "Leaves of the Fireweed," "Hair Seal's Ribs," and "Stick Fish Weir." Emmons noted that basketry designs predate European contact but are fundmentally unlike other types of Tlingit art. He speculated that the "geometric character of the design" had been borrowed, probably from interior Athapaskan quillwork (Emmons/deLaguna 1991:220-221).

121.

Beaded Disk by Madeline Krol, Athapaskan artist, Whittier, Alaska (b. 1946, Galena). Moose hide and glass beads. Private collection. 8 cm.

From Stone, Wood, and Skin to Paper

Paper was not available until European contact. It became even more available with the advent of formal schooling and emphasis on written communication. Alaska Natives, with their eye for innovation, must have seen many possibilities for applying the new techniques and materials almost immediately. Edward William Nelson, for example, related the following anecdote:

During one winter at St. Michael, a young Eskimo . . . came from the country of the Kaviak Peninsula and remained about the station. While there he took great pleasure in looking at the numerous illustrated papers we had, and would come day after day and borrow them; finally he came and asked me for a pencil and some paper, which I supplied him. Some days later I chanced to go to his tent, and found him lying prone upon the ground, with an old magazine before him, engaged in copying one of the pictures on the piece of paper. . . . He had done so well that I asked him if he could draw me some pictures of Eskimo villages and scenes. He agreed to try to do so and was furnished with a supply of pencils and paper. (1983 [1899]:197-98)

Near the turn of the century, Franz Boas used sketches by Qeqertuqdjuaq, a local artist, to illustrate folktales recounted in *The Central Eskimo* (1888). Waldemar Bogoras, while among the Chukchi in 1904-09, obtained a number of drawings from shamans and others. The attempt to transmit a sense of the intimate association of Native peoples with land, sea, and animals also led early anthropologists to commission Native cartography, although Native people rarely need maps themselves.

When formal education became compulsory for Alaska Native children, they were introduced, almost always unhappily, to long hours indoors and an inexplicable disregard for weather, seasons, and movements of animals (on which their lives had traditionally been based). They were also introduced to pencil and paper. Drawing and penmanship were emphasized in many districts, in part because teaching mainstream Western subjects was difficult in poorly equipped schools (Ray 1969:44). In some areas, the importance of signing one's work was introduced, and many teachers collected student work, using it to illustrate annual reports and personal memoirs.

A few teachers realized the importance of documenting Native life from their students' point of view, and most commented on the artistic abilities of local people. In Wales in the 1890s, government teachers Harrison Thornton and William T. Lopp, and later Susan Bernardi, all promoted drawing and painting. They used student works, including woodcuts, to illustrate the annual school newspaper, *The Eskimo Bulletin*. Sheldon Jackson included some of the drawings in his reindeer reports as well (Jackson 1895).

The close connection of contemporary graphic arts on paper with written communication, among Alaska Natives at least, may contribute to its lack of popularity, however. Whenever possible, most Native artists today still prefer to work with traditional materials—ivory, skin, and wood. The sophisticated development of graphic arts among the Tlingit and other Northwest Coast groups and the long history of two-dimensional works among Alaskan Eskimos would suggest that the switch to graphics on paper might be a natural one. Such a transition occurred in the Canadian Arctic—but not in Alaska.

122

Printmaking

A serious attempt to introduce printmaking in Alaska Native art was made during a nine-month series of multi-media workshops, the Designer-Craftsman Training Project under the Manpower Development and Training Act, sponsored nearly thirty years ago in Nome by the Indian Arts and Crafts Board (Ard 1982:270). The project, supervised by George Fedoroff, was managed by Inupiaq artist Ronald Senungetuk. Of the thirty students involved in the project, only one, Florence Nupok Malewotkuk, was a woman. Nupok, who had been encouraged by Otto Geist to produce ethnographic drawings while she was still a teenager, was the only student who had previous experience with graphics on paper (Ray 1969:64).

Later, the Visual Arts Center of Alaska made printing equipment available to Native artists, but most of the Native participants (all originally men) preferred to work in three dimensions and returned to large-scale sculpture. Canadian painter Gabriel Gely resided in Shishmaref during the early 1970s at the behest of the Community Enterprise Development Corporation (CEDC), where he encouraged many people to draw and to begin carving whalebone along with Melvin Olanna. Whalebone is now the primary material used in producing art in Shishmaref, but there is no corresponding industry in drawing or printmaking.

122.

"Shaman and Devil" by Kivetoruk Moses, Inupiaq artist from Shishmaref, Alaska. Anchorage Museum of History and Art, #82-100-6.

The Artists

The reasons why graphics production on paper has not been sustained among Alaska Native artists seem fairly clear. First, paper remains a less-than-comfortable material for most, who prefer to work on familiar surfaces in three dimensions. Second, the printmaking process requires much space, which is unavailable to most rural residents, and some processes need expensive equipment, usually installed at a university or other institution. Also, Native men traditionally worked and trained in communal settings such as the *kazigi* (men's house), usually in kin groups, while carving is often still done by younger men in a modified communal environment such as an abandoned village home. Printmaking is a more solitary endeavor, and perhaps therefore unpopular.

Finally, although the creation of the original design may be an invigorating moment, the printing process itself is somewhat tedious. And although problems of tedium and repetition could be resolved by working through an established press or by hiring an artist's representative, few Native artists pursue these options.

Native Alaskan graphic artists represent extremely diverse training and backgrounds. The style and medium used by each is clearly associated with the artist's time period and with the impact of European contact in the respective regions. Most "contemporary" artists, spanning the last two generations, have been formally trained. Other artists are generally called "traditional," although graphics production on paper is itself not a tradition.

In St. Michael at the turn of the century, Guy Kakarook was drawing and producing water-colors combined with crayon on paper, keeping his work in notebooks. He was probably influenced directly by Sheldon Jackson, General Agent of Education for the Territory of Alaska during the period 1885-1906 and a zealous Presbyterian missionary, who apparently provided Kakarook with government-issue art supplies (Ray 1969:46). Kakarook also engraved on ivory. In Nome during the same period, Angokwazhuk (Happy Jack) was a master engraver whose work on ivory was renowned up and down the Pacific coast.

Ray has noted that "the early school programs had little direct bearing on [later] successful commercial 'Eskimo art' on paper and animal hides" (1969:44) like that produced by Kivetoruk Moses, Robert Mayokuk, and George Ahgupuk two generations later. But all of these men were aware of the important associations of written communication and graphic arts with formalschooling and with newly introduced non-Native vocations—reindeer herding, teaching, and business. Kivetoruk Moses keenly recognized the value the written word held for non-Natives; for an extra five dollars, he would include a written story with his paintings (Ray 1969:56).

By the late 1930s, Moses, Ahgupuk (see Fig. 120), and Mayokuk were all well established and had become very prolific, selling primarily to collectors and to gift shops, which subsequently sold their work to tourists. Moses, the most painterly and best known of the group, remained in northwest Alaska, settling in Nome, where a market for Native art had been established since the Gold Rush. His experience is not isolated; many Inupiaq men turned to art production after working for many seasons away from their homes, often after a job-related injury forced their return.

George Ahgupuk and Robert Mayokuk moved on to urban Anchorage, where the souvenir market still dominates, and produced there successfully for the rest of their lives. Other men, including Melvin Olanna, sought alternative careers as artists because they had been handicapped by illness and feared (or were informed by elders) that they would not become proficient hunters (Fair 1993:16; Senungetuk 1990:5). As Olanna's success grew, he turned from ivory carving and occasional printmaking to large sculpture in wood, whalebone, or imported stone, establishing studio-residences in Shishmaref and Washington State.

123

123.

"Four Views" by Milo Minock, Inupiaq artist, Pilot Station, Alaska. Anchorage Museum of History and Art, #72-102-1.

Moses, Ahgupuk, Mayokuk, and other artists of their era are often described as "self-taught" (presumably through observation), but many were directly influenced by non-Natives—traders, teachers, and shopkeepers—although few records of these encounters remain. Kivetoruk Moses was first introduced to art supplies by the wife of a trader in Deering; he turned to art full-time after an injury sustained in a plane crash ended his varied career as hunter, reindeer herder, commercial fisherman, andentrepreneur in northwest Alaska. Moses served as a mentor to George Ahgupuk, his young brother-in-law, and to Harvey Pootoogooluk, now a prominent Shishmaref whalebone sculptor. He may also have influenced David Oakie and members of the Tingook family, also from the Shishmaref-Cape Espenberg area, as well as Wilbur Walluk (see Ray 1969:53-57). Ray has credited George Ahgupuk with instigating the shift from engraving on ivory to production on paper (1969:53), but the precedent for graphic art production was, by Aghupuk's productive years, already in place. Ahgupuk, along with Milo Minock of Pilot Station, turned graphics production back toward tradition by applying his original pen and ink drawings to smoothly processed skins—moose, caribou, and seal.

124,125

124, 125.

Native Artists from Siberia.
"Little girl with Dog" and "Reindeer Herder," 1990, by Et'ena Pavla Nikolaevicha, Chukchi artist from Topoliovka, Siberia (b. 1962). Student of Kilpalin (see Figs. 127, 128, 129).

Paper and ballpoint pen. Kamchatka Regional Museum, Russia, #28242 and #28243. 29.8 x 20.8 cm each.

126

126.

"The Hunt," 1970s, by Semion Nadein, Evenk artist from Sakhalin Island (1931-1982). Cut-out X-ray film. Sakhalin Regional Museum, Russia, #3345-3. 23x19 cm.

Nadein found his vocation as an artist while at a hospital as a young man, where he started to cut-out X-ray films with hunting scenes, reindeer, and Evenk folk tales.

127, 128, 129

127, 128, 129.

*"Myte," "Ania,"
and "Kutkiniako,"
1965, by Kirill
Vasilievich Kilpalin,
Koryak artist from
Topoliovka, Siberia
(1930-1991).*

*Paper, pencil, water-
color. Kamchatka
Regional Museum,
Russia, #30013, -14,
-17. 21x15 cm each.*

130.

*"Ukiu Vok Miut II
(King Island
Village)," 1963, by
Bernark Katexac,
Inupiaq artist, Nome,
Alaska (b. 1922,
King Island). Artist's
proof, woodcut.
Anchorage Museum
of History and Art,
#71-179-001.*

Bernard Katexac, Peter Seeganna, Teddy
Pullock, and Sylvester Ayek (see Fig. 117)
were all well-established King Island ivory
carvers who trained in printmaking at
various workshops statewide. Seeganna and
Ayek also worked in various other media
at Anchorage's Visual Arts Center. Seeganna,
a particularly promising artist, died of a
congenital heart condition in his mid-30s.
Teddy Pullock settled in Brevig Mission,
Alaska, where he is a carver. None of these
artists pursued printmaking for very
long, although Katexac and Seeganna executed various commissions on paper, as
did Melvin Olanna.

130

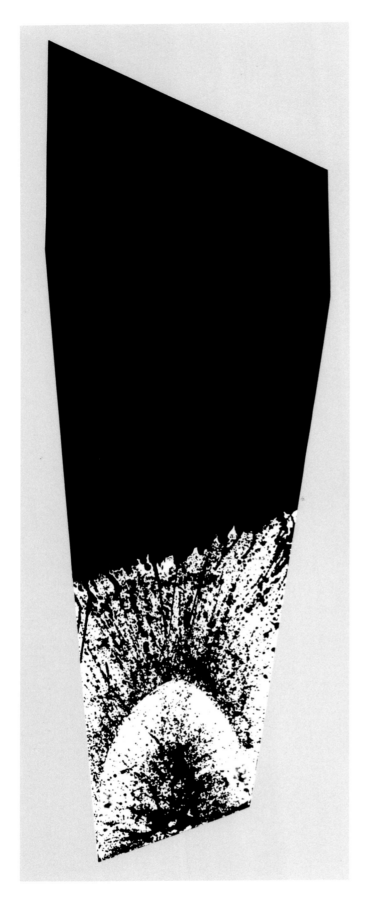

Other artists have pursued formal educations and are now established contemporary artists. Fred Anderson, an Aleut from Naknek who trained first as a painter, has produced many masks and notable sculptures and is now working on a massive series of drawings (Steinbright 1986:9).

Joseph Senungetuk is one of the best known graphic artists in Alaska. An Inupiaq who trained at the San Francisco Art Institute, Senungetuk is the author of *Give or Take a Century* (1970). This chronicle of his family's difficult move from Wales to Nome is illustrated with many of his prints and drawings. The younger brother of artist Ronald Senungetuk, he now concentrates primarily on masks, large-scale sculpture, and projects in ethnomusicology.

132

131.

"Transition," 1978, by Fred Anderson, Aleut artist, Naknek, Alaska (b. 1949, Naknek). Anchorage Museum of History and Art, #79-030-2.

132.

"A Dream in Anchorage," 1973, by Peter Seeganna, Inupiaq artist from King Island. Anchorage Museum of History and Art, #73-097-4.

131

Aleut Alvin Amason (see Fig. 116), a professor at the University of Alaska Fairbanks, is another prominent graphic artist. A noted painter who produces occasional prints, Amason frequently textures, builds up, and "adds on" to most of his pieces. He often writes on his work, thus combining graphics, sculpture, and oral tradition in an avant-garde blend that recalls other media and earlier traditions.

John Kailukiak (see Fig. 118), a Yupik artist who also participated in the Nome training project and graduated from the Rhode Island School of Design, is also an accomplished painter. Since his return to Toksook Bay several years ago, however, Kailukiak has concentrated on three-dimensional works, primarily masks. Ironically, maskmaking may be considered a more daring step on Nelson Island than works on paper, for masked dancing was once vigorously prohibited by Christian missionaries. As Kailukiak

points out: "The people in my area don't know whether to continue going back into making masks because of the shamanism [associated with them] . . . but the performances seem sort of incomplete without the masks" (Steinbright 1986:38). Comments by John Kailukiak, in fact, may clarify why graphics on paper have not become a popular medium for Alaska Native artists, why the conscious gesture toward tradition is so powerful and so ultimately satisfying:

Everything else [in my masks] is pretty much from home, even the colors we collect from the beaches and hills. . . . My designs are similar to those done before, those collected by Nelson and Curtis. My designs go back to that age. I've thought about using exotic wood for my masks but even though the product might be nice . . . it just doesn't seem right to work with wood different than driftwood. It's just that feeling . . . .

Hunting and artwork are the two main things in my life. It's hard for me to stay in the city. I've been tempted to go into the city in order to have better access to materials, but I don't want to go where I can't hunt.

–John Kailukiak (Steinbright 1986:38-39)

Acknowledgements

My thanks extend to George Ahgupuk, Alvin Amason, Saradell Ard, Michael Burwell, Steve Henrikson, Aldona Jonaitis, Marilyn Kwock, Dinah Larsen, Mary Larson, Melvin and Karen Olanna, Harvey Pootoogooluk, Dorothy Jean Ray, Shelley Reid and Dan Savard (Royal British Columbia Museum), Joseph Senungetuk, Ronald Senungetuk, Theresa Thibault, Walter Van Horn, Bill and Karen Workman, and many Native artists not mentioned here. Permission to use materials from the *Tradition, Innovation, Continuity* project, Alaska State Council on the Arts, comes from Jean Palmer, Acting Director. Most art pieces reproduced here were originally selected by curator Ronald Senungetuk for this project.

133.

*"The Silent Sea,"
1967, by Joseph
Senungetuk, Inupiaq
artist, Anchorage,
(b. 1940, Wales).
Anchorage Museum
of History and Art,
#85-069-1.*

133

Maps

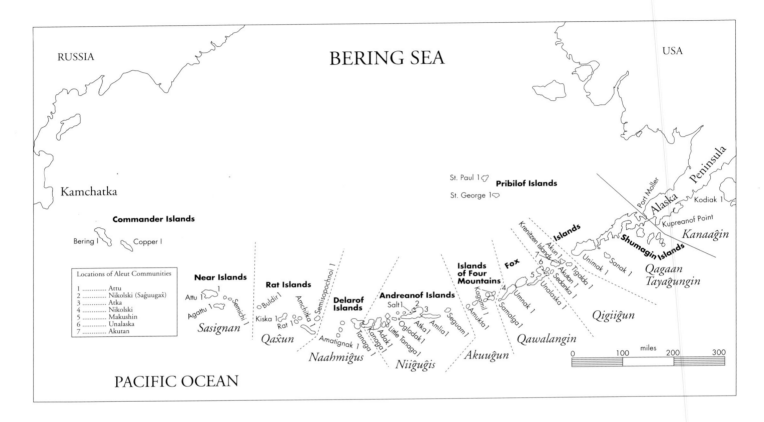

Map reproduced courtesy of the Alaska Native
Language Center, University of Alaska
Fairbanks, from Unungam Ungiikangin...
by Bergsland and Moses, 1990.

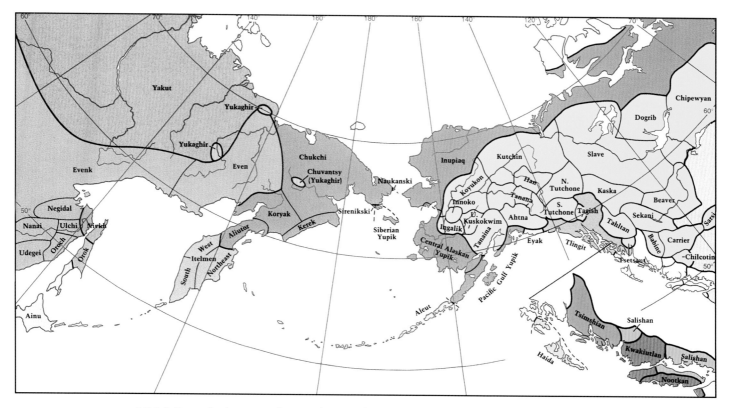

1994 Populations and Speakers of North Pacific Region Languages

Language Family		Language Name	Population	Speakers
Tungusic		Udegei	1,600	100
		Oroch	300	100
		Nanai/Goldi (Russia)	12,000	5,000
		Nanai/Goldi (China)	4,000	50
		Ulchi	3,200	500
		Orok	300	30
		Negidal	500	100
		Solon (China)	23,000	??
		Evenk/Tungus (Russia)	30,000	9,000
		Evenk/Tungus (Mongolia)	2,000	??
		Evenk/Tungus (Oroqen: China)	4,132	4,000
		Even/Lamut	17,000	7,500
Nivkh/Gilyak		Nivkh	4,500	400
Ainu		Ainu	16,000	10
Turkic		Yakut (Sov. Census 1985)	380,000	357,000
Yukaghir		Yukaghir	900	100
Chukotko-Kamchatkan		Itelmen/Kamchadal	1,500	100
		Koryak and Aliutor	9,000	4,600
		Aliutor subtotal	1,000	100
		Kerek	400	3
		Chukchi	15,000	10,000
Eskimo-Aleut		Inupiaq (Alaska)	13,500	3,500
		Sirenikski		1
		Siberian Yupik	2,000	1,300
		Chaplinski (Russia) subtotal	900	300
		St. Lawrence Is. (USA) subtotal	1,100	1,000
		Naukanski	450	70
		Central Alaskan Yupik	20,000	10,500
		Pacific Gulf Yupik	3,000	450
		Aleut (USA)	2,000	340
		Aleut (Russia)	300	5

Language Family		Language Name	Population	Speakers
Athapaskan-Eyak		Ahtna	500	80
		Tanaina	900	75
		Ingalik	275	40
		Innoko	200	12
		Koyukon	2,300	300
		Upper Kuskokwim	160	40
		Tanana	380	30
		Tanacross	220	65
		Upper Tanana	340	115
		Han	300	15
		Kutchin	3,000	700
		Eyak	5	2
Tlingit		Tlingit	11,000	575
Haida		Haida	2,200	55
Tsimshian		Coast Tsimshian	4,500	1000
		Nass-Gitksan	5,500	2,000
Wakashan (Kwakiutlan)		Haisla*	1,000	250
		Heiltsuk-Oowekyala*	1,200	450
		Kwakiutl*	3,300	1,000
Wakashan (Nootkan)		Nootka*	3,500	500
		Nitinat*	??	??
		Makah*	600	200
Salishan		Bella Coola*	700	150

Note: This map was adapted from *Crossroads of Continents: Cultures of Siberia and Alaska*, by William W. Fitzhugh and Aron Crowell, 1988. Figures have been updated by Igor Krupnik, Smithsonian Institution, and Michael Krauss, Alaska Native Language Center, University of Alaska Fairbanks, on the basis of Michael Krauss's report to UNESCO dated January 25, 1994, except for the figures marked with an asterisk, which are from 1977 data.

* Figures for 1977.

Bibliography

Achirgina-Arsiak, Tatiana
1992 Paianitok! *Etudes/Inuit/Studies* 16 (1-2):47-50.

Amason, Alvin
1982 The Contemporary Native Artist. *Native Arts Issues* 81/82, edited by Suzi Jones. Anchorage: Alaska State Council on the Arts. pp. 32-36.

Antropova, V.V., and V.G. Kuznetsova
1964 The Chukchi. *The Peoples of Siberia.* M.G. Levin and L.P. Potapov. Chicago and London: University of Chicago Press. Originally published in Russian in 1956 as *Narody Sibiri.* Moscow: ANSSSR. pp. 799-850.

Antropova, V.V.
1964 The Koryaks. *The Peoples of Siberia.* M.G. Levin and L.P. Potapov. Chicago and London: University of Chicago Press. Originally published in Russian in 1956 as *Narody Sibiri.* Moscow: ANSSSR. pp. 851-875.

Ard, Saradell (Frederick)
1970 An Analysis of Two-Dimensional Eskimo Pictorial Representation with Relevance for Art Teaching in Alaska. Unpublished Ph.D. dissertation, Columbia University, Department of Education.
1982 in William W. Fitzhugh and Susan Kaplan. *Inua: Spirit World of the Bering Sea Eskimo.* Washington, D.C.: Smithsonian Institution Press.

Arutiunov, Sergei A.
1988a. Chukchi: Warriors and Traders of Chukotka. *Crossroads of Continents: Cultures of Siberia and Alaska.* Edited by W.W. Fitzhugh and A. Crowell. Washington, D.C.: Smithsonian Institution Press. pp. 39-41.
1988b. Koryak and Itelmen: Dwellers of the Smoking Coast. *Crossroads of Continents: Cultures of Siberia and Alaska.* Edited by W.W. Fitzhugh and A. Crowell. Washington, D.C.: Smithsonian Institution Press. pp. 31-35.
1988c. Even: Reindeer Herders of Eastern Siberia. *Crossroads of Continents: Cultures of Siberia and Alaska.* Edited by W.W. Fitzhugh and A. Crowell. Washington, D.C.: Smithsonian Institution Press. pp. 35-38.

Berger, Thomas
1985 *Village Journey.* New York: Hill and Wang.

Bergsland, Knut
1994 *Aleut Dictionary.* Alaska Native Language Center, University of Alaska Fairbanks.

Bergsland, Knut, and Moses L. Dirks (editors)
1990 *Unangam Ungiikangin Kayux Tunusangin/Unangam Uniikangis Ama Tunuzangis/Aleut Tales and Narratives, collected 1909-1910 by Waldemar Jochelson.* Appendix: Aleut Lore Published in 1840 and 1846 by Ioann Veniaminov, re-edited by Knut Bergsland. Alaska Native Language Center, University of Alaska Fairbanks.

Black, Lydia T.
1973 The Nivkh (Gilyak) of Sakhalin and the Lower Amur. *Arctic Anthropology* 10 (1): 1-110.
1982 *Aleut Art.* Anchorage, Alaska: Aleutian/Pribilof Islands Association.
1988 Peoples of the Amur and Maritime Regions. *Crossroads of Continents: Cultures of Siberia and Alaska.* Edited by W.W. Fitzhugh and A. Crowell. Washington, D.C.: Smithsonian Institution Press.
1990 The Russian Conquest of Kodiak. Unpublished manuscript. University of Alaska Fairbanks, Department of Anthropology.
1991 *Glory Remembered: Wooden Headgear of Alaska Sea Hunters.* Juneau: Alaska State Museums.

Boas, Franz
1888 [1964] *The Central Eskimo.* 6th Annual Report of the Bureau of American Ethnology for the Years 1884-1885, pp. 399-669. Washington, D.C.: U.S. Government Printing Office. Reprinted by the University of Nebraska Press, 1964, with an introduction by Henry B. Collins.
1897 The Decorative Art of the Indians of the North Pacific Coast. *Bulletin of the American Museum of Natural History* 9: 123-176.
1903 The Jesup North Pacific Expedition. *The American Museum Journal* 3(5):72-119.
1905 The Jesup North Pacific Expedition. *Proceedings of the International Congress of Americanists,* 13th Session, New York 1902 pp. 91-100.

Bockstoce, J.R.
1986 *Whales, Ice, and Men; the History of Whaling in the Western Arctic.* Seattle: University of Washington Press.

Bogoras, Waldemar
1901 The Chukchi of Northeastern Asia. *American Anthropologist* 3:80-108.
1902 Folklore of Northeastern Asia, as Compared with that of Northwestern America. *American Anthropologist* 4:577-683.
1904-09 The Chukchee. *The Jesup North Pacific Expedition* 7, *Memoirs of the American Museum of Natural History.* Leiden/New York (Reprinted 1975, New York: AMS Press)
1910 Chukchee Mythology. *The Jesup North Pacific Expedition* 8(1), *Memoirs of the American Museum of Natural History.* Leiden/New York (Reprinted 1975, New York: AMS Press).
1913 The Eskimo of Siberia. *The Jesup North Pacific Expedition* 8(3), *Memoirs of the American Museum of Natural History.* Leiden/New York (Reprinted 1975, New York: AMS Press).

Burch, Ernest S., Jr.
1974 Eskimo Warfare in Northwest Alaska. *Anthropological Papers of the University of Alaska* 16:1-14.
1979 Indians and Eskimos in North Alaska, 1816-1977: a Study in Changing Ethnic Relations. *Arctic Anthropology* 16:123-151.
1978 Traditional Eskimo Societies in Northwest Alaska. in Alaska Native Culture and History, edited by Y. Kotani and W.B. Workman. *National Museum of Ethnology, Senri Ethnological Series* 4. Osaka, Japan. pp. 253-304. (Reprinted 1980).
1981 *The Traditional Eskimo Hunters of Point Hope, Alaska: 1800-1875.* Barrow, Alaska: North Slope Borough.
1984 Kotzebue Sound Eskimo. *Handbook of North American Indians* 5 (Arctic). Edited by D. Damas. Washington, D.C.: Smithsonian Institution. pp. 303-319.

Burch, E.S., Jr, and T.C. Corell
1972 Alliance and Conflict: Inter-regional Relations in North Alaska. *Alliance in Eskimo Society,* edited by D.L. Guemple. Seattle: University of Washington Press. pp. 17-39.

Carpenter, Edmund S.
1973 *Eskimo Realities.* New York: Holt, Rinehart and Winston.
1973 Some Notes on the Separate Realities of Eskimo and Indian Art. *The Far North, 2000 Years of American Eskimo and Indian Art,* edited by Henry Collins, Frederica de Laguna, Edmund Carpenter, and Peter Stone. Washington, D.C.: National Gallery of Art. pp. 281-289.

Chaussonnet, Valérie
1988 Needles and Animals: Women's Magic. *Crossroads of Continents: Cultures of Siberia and Alaska.* Edited by W.W. Fitzhugh and A. Crowell. Washington, D.C.: Smithsonian Institution Press. pp. 209-226.

Chaussonnet, Valérie, and Bernadette Driscoll
1994 The Bleeding Coat: The Art of North Pacific Ritual Clothing. *Anthropology of the North Pacific Rim.* Edited by W.W. Fitzhugh and V. Chaussonnet. Washington, D.C.: Smithsonian Institution Press. pp. 109-131.

Clark, Donald
1984 "Pacific Eskimo: Historical Ethnography." *Handbook of North American Indians.*Volume 5 (Arctic). Edited by D. Damas. Washington, D.C.: Smithsonian Institution Press.

Collins, Henry B., Frederica De Laguna, Edmund Carpenter, and Peter Stone
1973 *The Far North, 2000 Years of American Eskimo and Indian Art.* Washington, D.C.: National Gallery of Art.

Covarrubias, Miguel
1954 *The Eagle, the Jaguar, and the Serpent: Indian Art of the Americas; North America: Alaska, Canada, and the United States.* New York: Knopf.

Coyhis, Don
1993 Presentation at the Rural Development Workshop, "Seeds of Diversity." University of Alaska Fairbanks.

Crowell, Aron
1988a. Prehistory of Alaska's Pacific Coast. *Crossroads of Continents: Cultures of Siberia and Alaska.* Edited by W.W. Fitzhugh and A. Crowell. Washington, D.C.: Smithsonian Institution Press. pp. 130-140.
1988b. Dwellings, Settlements, and Domestic Life. *Crossroads of Continents, Cultures of Siberia and Alaska,* edited by W.W. Fitzhugh and A. Crowell. Washington, D.C.: Smithsonian Institution Press. pp. 194-208.

Cruikshank, Julie
1990 *Life Lived Like a Story.* Lincoln: University of Nebraska Press.

Dall, W.H.
1870 *Alaska and Its Resources.* Boston.

Damas, David (ed.)
1984 *Handbook of North American Indians.* Volume 5 (Arctic). Edited by D. Damas. Washington, D.C.: Smithsonian Institution Press.

Dauenhauer, Nora Marks, and Richard Dauenhauer
1987 *Haa Shuká, Our Ancestors: Tlingit Oral Narratives.* Seattle: University of Washington Press.
1990 *Haa Tuwunáagu Yís, For Healing Our Spirit: Tlingit Oratory.* Seattle: University of Washington Press.

Davis, Nancy Yaw
1984 Contemporary Pacific Eskimo. *Handbook of North American Indians.* Volume 5 (Arctic). Edited by D. Damas. Washington, D.C.: Smithsonian Institution Press.

de Laguna, Frederica
1972 Under Mount Saint Elias: The History and Culture of the Yakutat Tlingit. *Smithsonian Contributions to Anthropology* 7 (in three parts). Washington, D.C.: Smithsonian Institution Press.

de Laguna, Frederica, Francis A. Riddell, Donald F. McGeein, Kenneth S. Lane, J. Arthur Fried, and Carolyn Osborne
1964 *Archaeology of the Yakutat Bay Area, Alaska. Smithsonian Institution Bureau of American Ethnology, Bulletin* 192. Washington, D.C.: U.S. Government Printing Office.

Dikov, N.N.
1994 The Paleolithic of Kamchatka and Chukotka and the Problem of the Peopling of America. *Anthropology of the North Pacific Rim.* Edited by W.W. Fitzhugh and V. Chaussonnet. Washington, D.C.: Smithsonian Institution Press. pp. 87-96.

Duff, Wilson
1981 The World is as Sharp as a Knife: Meaning in Northwest Coast Art. *The World Is as Sharp as a Knife: An Anthology in Honour of Wilson Duff,* edited by Donald W. Abbott. Victoria, British Columbia: the British Columbia Provincial Museum. pp. 209-224. (Reprinted in *Indian Art Traditions of the Northwest Coast,* edited by Roy L. Carlson, 1983. Burnaby, British Columbia: Simon Frazer University. pp. 47-66).

Duncan, Kate
1984 *Some Warmer Tone: Alaska Athabascan Bead Embroidery.* Fairbanks, Alaska: University of Alaska Museum.
1988 *Northern Athapaskan Art: A Beadwork Tradition.* Seattle: University of Washington Press.

Dyson, George
1986 *Baidarka.* Edmonds, Washington: Alaska Northwest Publishing Company.

Emmons, George Thornton
1907 The Chilkat Blanket. *Memoirs of the American Museum of Natural History.* 3(4):229-277. New York.
1911 The Tahltan Indians. *University of Pennsylvania Museum Anthropological Publications* 4 (1): 1-120.
1916 The Whale House of the Chilkat. Anthropological *Papers of the American Museum of Natural History* 19 Part 1. pp. 1-33.
1991 *The Tlingit Indians.* Edited with additions by Frederica de Laguna; biography by Jean Low. Seattle: University of Washington.

Fair, Susan W.
1993 Alaska Native Art: History, Traditions, Transitions. *Arts From the Arctic.* Fairbanks: Institute of Alaska Native Arts and Anchorage Museum of History and Art.

Fienup-Riordan, Ann
1983 *Nelson Island Eskimos: Social Structure and Ritual Distribution.* Anchorage: Alaska Pacific University Press.
1987 The Mask: The Eye of the Dance. *Arctic Anthropology* 24 (2): 40-55.
1990 *Eskimo Essays: Yupik Lives and How We See Them.* New Brunswick and London: Rutgers University Press.

Fitzhugh, William W., and Valérie Chaussonnet (eds.)
1994 *Anthropology of the North Pacific Rim.* Washington D.C.: Smithsonian Institution Press.

Fitzhugh, William W., and Aron Crowell (eds.)
1988 *Crossroads of Continents: Cultures of Siberia and Alaska.* Washington, D.C.: Smithsonian Institution Press.

Fitzhugh, William W., and Susan Kaplan
1982 *Inua: Spirit World of the Bering Sea Eskimo.* Washington, D.C.: Smithsonian Institution Press.

Fortuine, Robert
1989 *Chills and Fever: Health and Disease in the Early History of Alaska.* Fairbanks: University of Alaska Press.

Giddings, J. Louis
1967 *Ancient Men of the Arctic.* New York: Alfred A. Knopf.

Goldman, I.
1975 *The Mouth of Heaven: An Introduction to Kwakuitl Religious Thought.* New York: Wiley.

Graburn, Nelson H.H.
1976 Eskimo Art: The Eastern Canadian Arctic. *Ethnic and Tourist Arts: Cultural Expressions from the Fourth World.* Edited by Nelson H.H. Graburn. Berkeley: University of California Press.

Hall, Edwin S., Jr., Margaret B. Blackman, and Vincent Rickard
1981 *Northwest Coast Indian Graphics.* Seattle: University of Washington Press.

Hall, Edwin
1984 Interior North Alaska Eskimo. *Handbook of North American Indians.* Vol. 5 (Arctic). Edited by D. Damas. Washington, D.C.: Smithsonian Institution Press. pp. 338-346.

Hallowell, A.I.
1926 Bear Ceremonialism in the Northern Hemisphere. *American Anthropologist* 28: 1-173.

Hatt, Gudmund
1969 Arctic Skin Clothing in Eurasia and America. An Ethnographic Study. *Arctic Anthropology* 5(2):1-132. (Originally published in Danish in 1914)

Haviland, William A.
1990 *Cultural Anthropology.* Fort Worth: Holt, Rinehart, and Winston, Inc.

Himmelheber, Hans
1987 [1938] *Eskimo Artists.* Zurich: Museum Rietberg.

Holm, Bill
1965 *Northwest Coast Indian Art: An Analysis of Form.* Seattle: University of Washington Press.
1981 Will the Real charles Edensaw Please Stand Up? The Problem of Attribution in Northwest Coast Indian Art. *The World is as Sharp as a Knife.* Victoria, British Columbia: British Columbia Provincial Museum. pp. 175-200.

1983 *The Box of Daylight. Northwest Coast Indian Art.* Seattle/London: University of Washington Press.
1987 *Spirit and Ancestor. A Century of Northwest Coast Indian Art at the Burke Museum.* Seattle: University of Washington Press.

Holm, Bill, and William Reid
1975 *Form and Freedom. A Dialogue on Northwest Coast Indian Art.* Houston: Institute for the Arts, Rice University.

Holmberg, Heinrich Johan
1985 *Holmberg's Ethnographic Sketches.* Falk (ed.). Fairbanks: University of Alaska Press. Originally published as *Ethnographische Skizzen ueber die Volker des Russischen Amerika* (1855-63).

Hrdlicka, Ales
1944 *The Anthropology of Kodiak Island.* Philadelphia: The Wistar Institute of Anatomy and Biology. Reprinted by AMS Press, New York.

Hughes, Charles
1984 Asiatic Eskimo: Introduction. *Handbook of North American Indians.* Volume 5. (Arctic). Edited by D. Damas. Washington, D.C.: Smithsonian Institution. pp. 243-261.

Institute of Alaska Native Arts
1984 *New Traditions: an Exhibition of Alaska Native Sculpture.* Fairbanks, Alaska.

Ivanov, S.V., M.G. Levin, and A.V. Smolyak
1964a. The Nanays. *The Peoples of Siberia.* Edited by M.G. Levin and L.P. Potapov. Chicago and London: University of Chicago Press. Originally published in Russian in 1956 as *Narody Sibiri.* Moscow: ANSSSR.
1964b. The Nivkhi. *The Peoples of Siberia.* M.G. Levin and L.P. Potapov. Chicago and London: University of Chicago Press. Originally published in Russian in 1956 as *Narody Sibiri.* Moscow: ANSSSR. pp. 767-787.

Jackson, Sheldon
1895 Report on Introduction of Domestic Reindeer into Alaska (1894). *53rd Congress, 2nd Session, Sen. Ex. Doc. 92.* Washington, D.C.: U.S. Government Printing Office.

Jochelson, Waldemar
1907 Past and Present Subterranean Dwellings of the Tribes of Northeastern Asia and Northwestern America. *Congrès International des Américanistes,* 15th session, Québec. pp. 115-128.
1908 The Koryak. *The Jesup North Pacific Expedition,* 6. *Memoirs of the American Museum of Natural History.* Leiden and New York. Reprinted in 1975 by AMS Press, New York.
1926 The Yukaghir and Yukaghirized Tungus. *The Jesup North Pacific Expedition,* 9. *Memoirs of the American Museum of Natural History.* Leiden and New York. Reprinted in 1975 by AMS Press, New York.
1933 *History, Ethnology, and Anthropology of the Aleut.* Washington, D.C.: Carnegie Institution of Washington.

Jonaitis, Aldona
1986 *The Art of the Northern Tlingit.* Seattle: University of Washington Press.
1988 *From the Land of the Totem Poles. The Northwest Coast Indian Art Collection at the American Museum of Natural History.* New York: American Museum of Natural History; and Seattle: University of Washington Press.

Jones, Dorothy Knee
1980 *A Century of Servitude: Pribilof Aleuts under U.S. Rule.* University Press of America.

Jones, Suzi (Ed)
1982 *Eskimo Dolls.* Anchorage, Alaska: Alaska State Council on the Arts.
1986 *The Artists Behind the Work.* Fairbanks, Alaska: University of Alaska Museum.

Jordan, Richard H., and Richard A. Knecht
1988 Archaeological Research on Kodiak Island, Alaska: The Development of Koniag Culture. *The Late Prehistoric Development of Alaska's Native People. Alaska Anthropological Association Monograph Series 4.* Edited by Shaw, Harritt, and Dumond.

Kan, Sergei
1989 *Symbolic Immortality: Tlingit Potlatch of the Nineteenth Century.* Washington, D.C.: Smithsonian Institution Press.

Knecht, Richard A., Sven Haakanson, and Shawn Dickson
n.d. Two Early Contact Sites on Kodiak Island, Alaska. Unpublished manuscript on file at the Kodiak Area Native Association.

Kodiak Area Native Association
1987 The History of the Traditional Native Village of Old Harbor and Its Government. Unpublished manuscript on file at the Kodiak Area Native Association.

Kotzebue, O.V.
1821 *A Voyage of Discovery into the South Sea and Beerings Straits, for the Purpose of Exploring a North-East Passage, Undertaken in the Years 1815-1818.* London: Longman, Hurst, Reese, Orme and Brown.

Krasheninnikov, Stepan P.
1972 *Exploration of Kamchatka* (Originally published in 1755). Portland: Oregon Historical Society.

Krauss, Michael E.
1983 Survival or Extinction for Alaska Native Languages. *Alaska Native News,* February. Anchorage, Alaska.
1988 Many Tongues—Ancient Tales. *Crossroads of Continents: Cultures of Siberia and Alaska.* Edited by W.W. Fitzhugh and A. Crowell. Washington, D.C.: Smithsonian Institution Press. pp. 145-150.
1994 Crossroads? A Twentieth-Century History of Contacts across the Bering Strait. *Anthropology of the North Pacific Rim.* Edited by W.W. Fitzhugh and V. Chaussonnet. Washington, D.C.: Smithsonian Institution Press. pp.365-379.

Kreynovich, E.A.
1979 The Tundra Yukaghir at the Turn of the Century. *Arctic Anthropology* 16 (1): 178-217.

Krupnik, Igor
1987 Bowhead versus Gray Whale in Chukotka Aboriginal Whaling. *Arctic* 40 (1): 16-32.
1988 Asiatic Eskimos and Marine Resources: A Case of Ecological Pulsation or Equilibrium? *Arctic Anthropology* 25 (1): 94-106.
1993 *Arctic Adaptations. Native Whalers and Reindeer Herders of Northern Eurasia.* Hanover and London: University Press of New England. Originally published as *Arkticheskaia Etnoekologiia* in 1989, Moscow: Nauka.

Lantis, Margaret
1938 The Alaska Whale Cult and Its Affinities. *American Anthropologist* n.s.40:438-464.
1947 Alaskan Eskimo Ceremonialism. *Monographs of the American Ethnological Society,* (New York) 11. New York: J.J. Augustin.
1984a Nunivak Eskimo. *Handbook of North American Indians* 5 (Arctic). Edited by D. Damas. Washington, D.C.: Smithsonian Institution. pp. 209-223.
1984b Aleut. *Handbook of North American Indians* 5 (Arctic). Edited by D. Damas. Washington, D.C.: Smithsonian Institution. pp. 161-184.

Laufer, Berthold
1902 The Decorative Art of the Amur Tribes. *The Jesup North Pacific Expedition,* 4. *Memoirs of the American Museum of Natural History.* Leiden and New York. Reprinted in 1975 by AMS Press, New York.

Lee, Molly
n.d. Eskimo/Inuit Architecture: a Survey of Indigenous House Form in the Pre-modern Period. Unpublished manuscript, Department of Anthropology, University of California, Berkeley.
1983 *Baleen Basketry of the North Alaska Eskimo.* Barrow, Alaska: North Slope Borough Planning Department.

Levin, M.G., and B.A. Vasil'yev
1964 The Evens. *The Peoples of Siberia.* Edited by M.G. Levin and L.P. Potapov. Chicago and London: University of Chicago Press. Originally published in Russian in 1956 as *Narody Sibiri.* Moscow: ANSSSR. pp. 670-690.

Lyons, W.J.
1964 The Koyukon Feast for the Dead. *Arctic Anthropology* pp. 133-146.

Mauss, Marcel
1990 *The Gift.* New York: W.W. Norton.

Merck, C.H.
1980 *Siberia and Northwestern America 1788-1792: The Journal of Carl Heinrich Merck.* Kingston, Ontario: The Limestone Press.

Moore Sharon, D., and Sophie M. Johnson
1986 Lena Sours. *The Artists Behind the Work.* Edited by Suzi Jones. Fairbanks: University of Alaska Museum.

Morrow, Phyllis
1984 It is Time for Drumming: a Summary of Recent Research on Yup'ik Ceremonialism. *Etudes/Inuit/Studies* 8 (Special Issue):113-140.

Murdoch, John
1892 Ethnological Results of the Point Barrow Expedition. *9th Annual Report of the Bureau of American Ethnology for the Years 1887-1888.* Washington, D.C. (Reprinted 1988 with Introduction by William W. Fitzhugh, Classics of Smithsonian Anthropology Series, Smithsonian Institution).

Nabokov, Peter, and Robert Easton
1989 *Native American Architecture.* New York: Oxford University Press.

Nagishkin, Dmitrii
1980 *Folktales of the Amur: Stories from the Russian Far East.* New York: Harry N. Abrams, Inc./Leningrad: Aurora Art Publisher.

Nelson, Edward W.
1983 [1899] *The Eskimo About Bering Strait.* Bureau of American Ethnology Annual Report, Vol. 1. Reprinted Washington, D.C.: Smithsonian Institution Press, 1983, with introduction by William W. Fitzhugh.

Okladnikov, Aleksei P.
1981 *Ancient Art of the Amur Region.* (Also entitled: Art of the Amur, Ancient Art of the Russian Far East). Leningrad: Aurora.

Olson, Wallace
1991 *The Tlingit: An Introduction to Their Culture and History.* Auke Bay, Alaska: Heritage Research. Distributed by Sealaska Heritage Foundation.

Paul, Frances
1944 *Spruce Root Basketry of the Alaska Tlingit.* Washington, D.C.: Education Division, Indian Service.

Pullar, Gordon L.
1992 Ethnic Identity, Cultural Pride, and Generations of Baggage: A Personal Experience. *Arctic Anthropology* 29 (2). University of Wisconsin Press.

Ray, Dorothy Jean
1969 Graphic Arts of the Alaskan Eskimo. *Native American Arts* 2. Washington, D.C.: Indian Arts and Crafts Board.
1975 *The Eskimos of Bering Strait, 1650-1898.* Seattle: University of Washington Press. Reprinted 1992
1977 *Eskimo Art: Tradition and Innovation in North Alaska.* Seattle: University of Washington Press.
1981 *Aleut and Eskimo Art. Tradition and Innovation in South Alaska.* London: C. Hurst & Company.
1984 Bering Strait Eskimo. *Handbook of North American Indians* 5 (Arctic). Edited by D. Damas. Washington, D.C.: Smithsonian Institution. pp. 285-302.

Ray, Dorothy Jean, and Alfred A. Blaker
1967 *Eskimo Masks: Art and Ceremony.* Seattle/London: University of Washington Press.

Schevill, Margot Blum
1986 *Costume as Communication.* Bristol, R.I.: Haffenreffer Museum of Anthropology; Seattle: University of Washington Press.

Schneider, Harold K.
1989 *Economic Man.* Salem: Sheffield Publishing Company.

Schuster, Carl
1951 Joint Marks: A Possible Index of Cultural Contact between America, Oceania, and the Far East. *Royal Tropical Institute* 39: 4-51. Amsterdam.

Senungetuk, Joseph E.
1970 *Give or Take a Century: An Eskimo Chronicle.* San Francisco: Indian Historian Press.

Senungetuk, Ronald W.
1990 Eskimo Graphics Exhibit. Unpublished manuscript submitted to the Alaska State Museum and the Institute of Alaska Native Arts as an exhibition plan.

Service, Elman R.
1978 The Reindeer Tungus of Siberia. *Profiles in Ethnology.* New York: Harper and Row. pp. 113-131.

Shavanda, B.
1987 The Cycle of Collective Grief. Unpublished manuscript. University of Lethbridge.

Simeone, William
1990 Identity, History, and the Northen Athabaskan Potlatch. Unpublished dissertation. Ontario: McMaster University.

Smith, Dorothy A., and Leslie Spier
1927 The Dot and Circle Design in Northwestern America. *Society of Americanists* (NS) 19: 47-55.

Spencer, Robert F.
1959 *The North Alaskan Eskimo: A Study in Ecology and Society.* Washington, D.C.: Smithsonian Institution.
1984 North Alaska Coast Eskimo. *Handbook of North American Indians.* Vol. 5 (Arctic). Edited by D. Damas. Washington, D.C.: Smithsonian Institution Press. pp. 320-337.

Steinbright, Jan (ed.)
1986 *Alaskameut '86.* Fairbanks: Institute of Alaska Native Arts.

Sullivan, Robert J., S.J.
1936 The Ethnology of the Ten'a Indians of Interior Alaska. Master of Arts dissertation at the Catholic University of America, Washington, D.C.

Swanton, John R.
1908 Social Condition, Beliefs, and Linguistic Relationship of the Tlingit Indians. *Annual Report, Bureau of American Ethnology, 1904-1905.* 26:391-485.

VanStone, James W.
1974 *Athabaskan Adaptations.* Illinois: Harlan Davidson, Inc.

Vaughan, Thomas, and Bill Holm
1982 *Soft Gold, the Fur Trade and Cultural Exchange on the Northwest Coast of America.* Portland: Oregon Historical Society.

Voblov, I.K.
1959 Eskimo Ceremonies (translated by Charles Hughes). *Anthropological Papers of the University of Alaska* 7 (2): 71-90.

Watanabe, Hitoshi
1972 The Ainu. *Hunters and Gatherers Today.* Edited by M. Bichieri. New York: Holt, Rinehart, and Winston. pp. 448-484.

Yugtun Qaneryaramek Calivik / Yupik Language Center
n.d. Unpublished manuscript. Bethel, Alaska: Kuskokwim College.

Zimmerly, David W.
1986 *Qajaq; Kayaks of Siberia and Alaska.* Juneau Alaska: Division of State Museums.

Contributors

Aleut

Unangan (Aleut) storyteller **Barbara Švarný Carlson** was raised in Unalaska and is of the Qawalangin Tribe. She has a passion for the preservation of Unangan culture with an emphasis on the oral tradition. Intertwining the arts of dance, tattooing, and storytelling, she captivates young and old alike with tales from a time "so long ago that things were very different from the way they are today."

Tlingit

Nora Marks Dauenhauer was born in 1927 in Juneau, Alaska, and was raised in Juneau and Hoonah, as well as on the family fishing boat and in seasonal subsistence sites around Icy Strait, Glacier Bay, and Cape Spencer. Her first language is Tlingit; she began to learn English when she entered school at the age of eight. She has a B.A. in anthropology (Alaska Methodist University, 1976) and is internationally recognized for her fieldwork, transcription, translation, and explication of Tlingit oral literature. Her poetry, prose, and drama have been widely published and anthologized. She is Principal Researcher in Language and Cultural Studies at Sealaska Heritage Foundation in Juneau. She has four children and thirteen grandchildren.

Richard Dauenhauer, born (1942) and raised in Syracuse, N.Y., has lived in Alaska since 1969. From 1981 to 1988 he served as Alaska's seventh poet laureate. He holds a B.A. degree in Slavic languages, an M.A. in German, and a Ph.D. in comparative literature. He has taught at Alaska Methodist University and Alaska Pacific University in Anchorage and teaches part-time at the University of Alaska-Southeast in Juneau. Three volumes of his poetry have been published, and he is widely recognized as an editor and translator. He is Director of Language and Cultural Studies at Sealaska Heritage Foundation, Juneau. In 1991 Nora and Richard Dauenhauer shared an American Book Award for their Tlingit work.

Athapaskan

Bernice Joseph is an Athapaskan from Nulato, Alaska, and currently resides in Fairbanks. She has a B.B.A. in business administration (University of Alaska Fairbanks, 1989) and is noted for her involvement in cultural programs with the Native community in Fairbanks. She is the Program Officer of Education at Doyon Foundation in Fairbanks. Bernice is married and has two children.

Miranda Wright, a graduate student of anthropology at the University of Alaska Fairbanks, serves as vice-president of Keepers of the Treasures Alaska. A Koyukon Athapaskan born at the family campsite, Tson Yil, Miranda is involved in cultural preservation and perpetuation efforts of the peoples of Alaska. She served as the education coordinator for the *Crossroads Alaska* project.

Melinda Chase, formerly of Tanana Chiefs Conference village government services, is currently employed by the University of Alaska Interior Campus as rural education coordinator for the Galena subregion. She is involved with the Alaska Native Leadership Project and the Anvik Historical Society.

Alutiiq

Gordon L. Pullar is director of the Alaska Native Human Resource Development Program, College of Rural Alaska, University of Alaska Fairbanks, and the President of the national board of Keepers of the Treasures: Cultural Council of American Indians, Alaska Natives, and Native Hawaiians. He is a past president of the Kodiak Area Native Association.

Richard Knecht is an archeologist and the director of the Alutiiq Museum for the Kodiak Area Native association in Kodiak, Alaska. Originally from northern Michigan, he worked on archeological projects throughout the eastern U.S. before coming to Alaska as a student of the late Richard Jordan in 1983. He has directed numerous excavations throughout the Kodiak archipelago and is currently completing a Ph.D. in anthropology from Bryn Mawr College.

Inupiaq

Jana Harcharek is Inupiaq from Barrow, Alaska, where she was raised and taught to appreciate the value of learning both the Inupiaq ways and the ways of the western world. She has been involved in language and cultural preservation for a number of years, recently as liaison officer for the North Slope Borough Commission on Inupiat History, Language, and Culture. She is Chairperson of the Keepers of the Treasures Alaska, an organization devoted to reclaiming, revitalizing, and perpetuating the diverse cultures of the peoples of Alaska.

Rachel Craig is Inupiat Ilitqusiat Coordinator for Alaska's Northwest Arctic Borough, handling questions and issues relating to Inupiaq culture. She has collected oral history among Inupiaq elders, helped to develop the Inupiaq language curriculum for Northwest Arctic Borough schools, and is involved in various projects to preserve Inupiaq language, dance, and craft-making skills. She has also served in the Alaska Humanities Forum and the Alaska Historical Society, and is a board member of Keepers of the Treasures Alaska.

Yupik

Larry Kairaiuak is also known by his Yupik name, Apacuar. He was born in Bethel, Alaska, and grew up in the village of Chefornak, where Yupik was his first language. He holds a B.A. in history (University of Alaska Fairbanks, 1991) and has worked in the Fairbanks North Star Borough School District for the Alaska Native Education Program.

Darlene Orr is a Siberian Yupik now residing in Nome, Alaska, where she teaches Russian and her Native language at the local college. She also carries out linguistic fieldwork in Siberian Native languages on the verge of extinction for the Alaska Native Language Center, University of Alaska Fairbanks.

Siberian Peoples

Igor Krupnik is a research anthropologist at the Arctic Studies Center of the Smithsonian Institution in Washington, D.C. Born and educated in Russia, he spent almost twenty years studying the cultural legacy and traditional economies of Siberian Native people. He has authored numerous publications both in Russian and English: his *Arctic Adaptations: Whalers and Reindeer Herders of Northern Eurasia* was published in 1993 by the University Press of New England. At the Smithsonian, Dr. Krupnik is involved in several international research projects that focus on cultural preservation and change, and the environmental knowledge of circumpolar people.

Archeology

William W. Fitzhugh is the project director for *Crossroads Alaska* and director of the Arctic Studies Center at the Smithsonian Institution, where he has served as chairman of the Department of Anthropology. A specialist in archeology and anthropology of Arctic regions, he has conducted fieldwork in Labrador, Baffin Island, and other northern areas, including, recently, the Yamal Peninsula in Siberia. Special interests include prehistory and environmental archeology, circumpolar maritime adaptations, and culture contacts. He has produced several exhibitions, including *Inua* and *Crossroads of Continents*. Recent books include *Anthropology of the North Pacific Rim*, co-edited with Valérie Chaussonnet, and *Archeology of the Frobisher Voyages*.

Ethnology

Valérie Chaussonnet, Curator of *Crossroads Alaska*, has been associated with the Arctic Studies Center at the Smithsonian Institution since 1986. A member of the *Crossroads of Continents* curatorial team, she contributed a chapter on clothing to the exhibition catalogue and translated the Russian chapters into English. She has lectured in the United States and Canada on Arctic clothing and the peoples of Siberia. Valérie was co-editor of *Anthropology of the North Pacific Rim* with William W. Fitzhugh. She lives in Washington, D.C., with her husband and son.

Alaska Native Graphic Art

Susan W. Fair is an independent scholar, writer, and folklorist who lives in Eagle River, Alaska. She has worked intensively with Alaska Native artists for twenty years and has published numerous essays on Native art. The University of Alaska Press is about to publish her book on tradition, and she is presently working on an ethnohistory of northwest Alaskan Inupiat for the National Park Service.